VIGILANTISM
IN AMERICA

Also by Arnold Madison

VANDALISM:
The Not-So-Senseless Crime

VIGILANTISM
IN AMERICA

by Arnold Madison

A Clarion Book

THE SEABURY PRESS · New York

E
179
M18

Second Printing

Copyright © 1973 by Arnold Madison

Designed by Paula Wiener
Printed in the United States of America

LIBRARY OF CONGRESS CATALOGING IN PUBLICATION DATA

Madison, Arnold.
  Vigilantism in America.

  Bibliography: p. 171
  1. Vigilance committees—History. 2. Violence—
United States. I. Title.
E179.M18   322.4′4′0973   73–6953
ISBN: 0-8164-3102-7

For Jane Zaklan:
intelligent, imaginative,
and indomitable

Contents

VIGILANTISM
IN AMERICA

Introduction:
"... we'll handle it
ourselves!"

Fear has become second nature to most Americans to-day. The habit of fear grew subtly, noticed by an observant few when drugs left the ghettos and prospered in the blossoming markets of suburbia and when another market began drawing ever-increasing profits: locks and firearms.

Now a day rarely goes by when a chilling doubt about our personal safety or the well-being of loved ones doesn't flicker through our minds. Possibly it appears as a momentary pause as we're leaving home for a neighborhood movie theater. Will our possessions be intact upon our return? Even the least cognizant are jarred by the constant reminders in daily newspapers and trade journals:

RURAL CRIME SPREADS FEAR AND DISTRUST
—*The New York Times*

1

IN OUR CITIES, 1 PERSON IN 29
IS EITHER MURDERED,
MUGGED, ROBBED OR RAPED
—*Variety*

Yes, the fear is there, gnawing at us. In April 1972 results were released of a nationwide Gallup poll of 1,478 persons over the age of eighteen that dealt with crime. Thirty-five per cent of those interviewed believed there was more crime in their communities than there had been a year before. There was a 14 per cent increase over a 1968 poll showing women who were afraid to go out alone at night. Nationally, there was a 10 per cent increase among both men and women who said they were afraid.

People have become ultra-aware of crime and are frightened. But when they turn for help, they are confronted with other disturbing facts. "Public complaints of police corruption are reported to have tripled in a year," stated *The New York Times* in November 1971. But it isn't only the police who seem to be failing us. Reports about blatantly corrupt politicians and bureaucratic government at all levels follow one upon the other. In the same Gallup poll quoted above, 25 per cent of the people questioned thought that a major reason for the increase in crime was that the laws were too lenient. Distrust of our legal system itself appears to be spreading.

So fear is slowly blending with the feeling that our interests are being ignored or, at best, not served well.

A dangerous mixture of emotions, indeed, needing only a catalyst to produce a violent reaction.

The precedent for citizen action was set and glorified in our history. Did the colonists sit back when excessive taxes were imposed on them? Did the pioneers put up with horse thieves and cattle rustlers while awaiting action by territorial courts? No! Vigilantes organized, and they eradicated the problems! Justice was swift, cruel, and often misdirected, but the vigilantes did their work *fast*.

Although they derive from the French and Latin word *vigilant*—meaning alertly watchful; attentive to discover and avoid danger or to provide for safety—the words "vigilante" and "vigilantism" were both coined in the United States. And although there have been instances òf what might be called vigilantism in other times and other regions of the world, this book will focus on the origins and spread of vigilantism in America.

Today, neo-vigilante bands are springing up all over the United States, all sharing an impatience with some existing situation and all demanding immediate action. A *vigilante group* is one that forms with a common desire to change a certain condition. The vigilantes feel that the end justifies the means. To attain their end they will employ what seems to them the most effective method, with little regard for either the existing laws or the basic rights of human beings. In fact, vigilantes appear to believe that the people who offend them have no rights. This seems a curious philosophy for people living in a democracy; it may stem from the vigilantes' often fanatical certainty that they are completely in the right.

Vigilantes have always come in all sizes and shapes. Perhaps this is what is so deceiving about vigilantism and why so many unsuspecting people become involved with vigilante bands. All such organizations are not the lynch-mob variety. A group of peace-loving individuals can unobtrusively infringe upon another person's rights as much as a gang of loud-mouthed racists.

There are also individual vigilantes. Newspaper articles describe the increasing number of storekeepers who now keep guns under their counters. In Greenville, South Carolina, Courtney Lipscomb, an insurance salesman, was photographed by *Life* magazine, gun in hand, picking up his late afternoon paper as he arrived home from work. Lipscomb keeps a revolver in his car because he believes drug-related crimes have created "the most awful threat we ever imagined."

Residents of the Borough of Queens, New York City, may not think of themselves as related to a hooded, vigilante mob of the past, but their handling of a recent local problem puts them under the same definition. The point of controversy centered in a neighborhood park at 78th Avenue off Grand Central Parkway. The residents claimed that the wooded section was a nightly haven for homosexuals and asked the police to clear the area of the "undesirables." Complaints were also registered with the Commissioner of Parks and with New York City Mayor John Lindsay. An assistant to the mayor, David Love, wrote to the residents saying that the mayor's office would "immediately take steps" to improve the situation by trying to get better lighting and more police protection in the park. And the police patrols *were* beefed up.

These actions were not sufficient to allay the fears of the residents, however. Only the complete removal of the offending individuals could soothe their outrage. Obviously, this was not going to be accomplished by an outside agency, so the residents decided to handle the problem themselves. On the night of June 18, 1970, a group of men armed themselves with hatchets and axes and invaded the park. Systematically, they chopped down the trees and bushes they felt provided a shield for the homosexuals.

A passerby, who identified himself only as Glen Winchell, an assumed name that he used to protect himself from retaliation by the ax-swinging vigilantes, saw the illegal destruction. He phoned the 112th Police Precinct in nearby Maspeth. According to Mr. Winchell, a patrol car arrived on the scene about an hour after his call. Mr. Winchell claimed the officers merely chatted with the men who were cutting down the trees and then left, making no arrests.

Another Queens resident who witnessed the same vigilante action, wrote her experiences of that night to Mayor Lindsay, to the Police Commissioner, to the Park Commissioner, and to *The New York Times*. Joan Luxenburg and a male friend were riding by the park when they saw a man chopping down a tree while others stood by watching. Miss Luxenburg wrote: "My friend said to the man, 'I saw you chop down that tree and I'll remember you.' " The vigilante swung his ax and shouted,

"I'll *remember* you!" at which she and her friend quickly rolled up the car windows. The vigilante made another threatening gesture. Immediately, Joan Luxenburg and her companion drove to the front entrance of the park, where they found a different police car from the one Glen Winchell had notified. When the information about the destruction of public property was related to these policemen, the officers ignored it. The law-enforcement officials told Joan Luxenburg and her companion that the citizens of the community "were doing a job which the police were not able to do to the satisfaction of the community."

What were the results of this vigilante action? The most easily discerned was the destruction. Fifteen dogwood trees, eleven London planes, a number of wild cherry trees, and other greenery were gone. The cost of replacing them was placed at $15,000. The harm done by this citizen brand of justice far surpassed a monetary figure, however. More frightening is the disregard of one group's rights by another. Shortly after the vigilantes destroyed the park, the Civil Liberties Union urged "that the Police Commissioner and the Mayor make it clear to all members of the police force that homosexuals have as much right to the parks as heterosexuals and are entitled to the same degree of protection by the police."

What if a different group had decided they wanted the park for their exclusive use? Youngsters, for instance, might have wrecked the benches and greenery so that they would have a large, cleared space for their ball games. Or whites might have become alarmed if blacks were enjoying the pleasures of the park. And what if the group being forced from the area was not as passive as the homosexuals were on that occasion? Would there then have been retaliatory attacks on individuals? Deaths?

Death nearly resulted from the efforts of vigilantes in California where Peter G. Bohmer was employed as an economics professor at San Diego State College. Bohmer was thought to lean to the Left politically and to prefer his own life-style off campus. He and a group of seven young men and women lived together, calling themselves the Ocean Beach Collective. But Professor Bohmer's purported political ideology was the catalyst that produced a reaction in the SAO (Secret Army Organization).

The SAO is a right-wing paramilitary group made up of former servicemen in the San Diego area. These men feel that while they were in uniform they gave up years of their lives and risked death to defend this country. Now at home with their families, they thought they saw another danger to the United States, to its Constitution, and to democracy itself. Subversives, they believed, were everywhere, undermining our government, preparing this country for takeover by a foreign country. The veterans believed every good citizen had to do something to save America. For these men the thing to do was to join the SAO and arm themselves with information about any individual or group they felt to be Communist. The organization tried to educate others by distributing flyers containing their accusations. One pamphlet handed out in December 1971 concerned Professor Peter Bohmer: "To any of our readers who may care to look up this RED SCUM and say hello, here is some information that may help." The pamphlet listed Bohmer's address, physical description, and the make and license number of his automobile.

Phone calls and letters threatening Bohmer's life began arriving at his home. The police were notified, but did nothing until January 6, 1972. On that night, while Bohmer attended a basketball game, a light-blue Plymouth Valiant pulled up in front of Bohmer's house. Two shots smashed a house window. One bullet wounded twenty-two-year-old Paula Tharp who lived in the house. The car and would-be murderers vanished into the night.

Miss Tharp recovered quickly, having been wounded only in the right elbow. For a while the police gave Bohmer extra protection, as did San Diego State College. An article, sometimes two, appeared in most of the major California papers. Then the incident was forgotten, pushed from people's minds by the next headline.

Yet the SAO and equally dangerous right- and left-wing organizations continue to function in this country. Granted that the concern of the members of these groups is real, one still wonders what it is they are trying to protect by encouraging people to attack those of different political beliefs? Certainly not the Bill of Rights? And if the attempts at education and murder-by-proxy fail, is the next development to send out armed assassins? Fear has convinced the vigilantes that their enemy has no civil rights. Only one more step is needed for these people to be assured that the person or persons they see as their enemy have no right to live.

And therein lies the true danger of vigilantism. People genuinely concerned about some facet of society that they feel threatens their lives, property, or way of life become so determined to eliminate this factor that they will do anything—except follow legal procedures —to effect that change. A vast difference exists between a community-action program that follows democratic and legal procedures in an attempt to better an area and a vigilante group that works to get rid of that same malevolence by any means possible. Vigilantes mouth words about law and order and moral decay, but almost without exception, they display an arbitrary attitude toward law and a frightening disrespect of human liberties.

Many people who would not normally take the law into their own hands are attracted by this law-and-order call to action. And with good reason. Law and order promises security and safety. Everything would have its place, duties, limitations if law and order governed supreme. The goal of *total* law and order, however, is Utopian. Admittedly a sort of peace would reign. But would everyone be safe from the greedy and unscrupulous? A climate of thorough law and order existed in Nazi Germany. Crime practically disappeared, but so did every opposing political party and the rights of the ordinary citizen. The dream for complete law and order is an impossible one and may have to be tempered. Yet most people feel this desire for law and order deep within themselves.

Justice is the people's attempt to define a system of law and order that is fair to all. An ancient Roman law code stated: "Justice is the constant and perpetual wish to render everyone his due." The Roman sentiments are not far removed from the popular concept Americans share with people of other countries that "my home is my castle." Vigilantes have broadened this idea to include anything affecting their life-styles. If a threat comes, vigilantism acts on the principle that the rules of democratic society can be overlooked in the battle against the enemy. "Vigilantism is a violent sanctification of the deeply cherished values of life and property," concluded Richard Maxwell Brown in *Violence in America*.

This feeling coupled with an overinterpretation of the meaning of liberty has been a basic cause of vigilantism all through American history. Vigilantes always believe that they have the liberty and the right to take the law into their own hands. They fail to see that freedom imposes responsibilities. For instance, each person has a duty to be certain that his or her pursuit of freedom does not infringe upon another's civil rights. Vigilantes do not or will not observe this aspect of living in a democracy.

VIGILANTISM
IN AMERICA'S
PAST

1

The Threat of
Colonial Living

Salem, Massachusetts,
and the Back Country
of South Carolina

Vigilantism is indigenous to America, having sprouted
almost with the Pilgrim's first corn crop. Though Euro-
pean colonization had been going on for many years,
expansion elsewhere in the world failed to create anything resembling our vigilante tradition. Possibly it may
be that the colonies here were settled by men determined
to escape an insufferable life-style. Anything endanger-
ing the whole purpose of the venture had to be relent-
lessly rooted out lest it in some way return them to the
conditions they had escaped. Colonies on other conti-
nents were usually economically motivated or else were
havens for deported criminals. Whatever the case, America may be credited with forging a new instrument to
preserve law and order.

Whether historical or contemporary, vigilantism rises
to fight a threat that may be to moral values, to life, or

to property. The main thrust of vigilantism then becomes an effort to reestablish the more traditional values of a community. Or vigilantism can be a means for the Establishment to maintain its position of power. The danger is clear. Vigilantes operate outside the law, without restraints; thus injustices and extremism are almost a certainty as an outcome of their activities.

One of the earliest examples of vigilantism in America, though the term "vigilante" had not yet been coined at the time, occurred in Salem, Massachusetts, in 1692.

In the early 1600s a group of thirty colonists abandoned their efforts to eke a living from the poor soil of Cape Ann, Massachusetts, and moved southward along the coast to a place the Indians called Naumkeag. There they founded the village of Salem. In 1629 New England's first Puritan church was built in the settlement. As years went by the community leaders were also the most powerful members of the Puritan sect. Whether in dealing with matters of farming, shipbuilding, commerce, or religion, the word of these church leaders was absolute. Salem was clearly stratified economically, socially, and in terms of influence. A well-defined system of law and order reigned.

Salem was to learn, however, what most communities have had to accept throughout the history of the United States. Nothing is forever. Times and tempers change; newcomers arrive; older members of an area either die or move away. So it was with Salem. After about twenty years of religious and civil power, the Puritan theocracy was breaking down. Two generations of colonial Americans had matured. New settlers had entered Salem and were not willing to accept the stringent dictates of the Puritan dogma. The mood was one of quiet social rebellion. The nearer the Puritan rule came to the end, the more desperately it demanded conformity.

There was, too, a historical precedent for what was about to happen. Thirty years before, four Bostonian Quakers had been hanged for heresy by the Puritans.

So everything was primed for the madness that was to sweep Salem. Those in power, finding that their empire was tottering, were struggling to keep control. In nearby Boston men not unlike them had resorted to hangings as a means of maintaining their power.

In 1692 the Salem household of the Reverend Samuel Parris contained, among others, his imaginative eleven-year-old niece, Abigail Williams and a slave named Tituba, who was from Barbados. Tituba constantly told tales about voodoo, black magic, and devils. The stories had more effect on impressionable Abigail than did Parris' sermons. One day Abigail and a few young friends began screaming that they were being bitten by demons. They barked like dogs and threw themselves on the floor as if they were suffering convulsions.

Tituba and two elderly companions, Sarah Good and Sarah Osborne, were arrested for witchcraft. A confession was forced from Tituba that indicted her two friends. The Barbadian slave embellished her story by describing the bloodred cats and the yellow birds that were her familiars, or demons in animal disguise.

Two old and respected churchwomen denounced the children's stories as products of twisted minds. Abigail

and her friends accused them next and had the satisfaction of seeing the women put on trial.

The children were in their glory. Anyone they disliked or any people who would not cower before their
new power would be pointed out as witches. The girls
quickly became the center of Salem's attention and had
more influence than many adult members of the community. The church leaders supported them, hoping
that the atmosphere of fear enveloping Salem would
bring complete obedience to Puritan rule. The vigilantes cloaked their activities under the disguise of legal
procedures, but their flagrant misuse of power places
their actions squarely in the category of vigilantism.
And the Salem vigilantes went about their task with
enthusiasm.

More arrest warrants were issued . . .

> . . . for high suspicion of Sundry acts of Witchcraft
> donne or Committed by them upon the bodys of Abi-
> gaile Williams, and John Indian both of Mr. Saml.
> Parris his famyly of Salem Village and Mary Walcott
> . . . and Ann Putnam of Salem Village. Whereby great
> hurt and dammage hath benne donne to the Bodys of
> persons above named.

The Salem jail became filled. A new court was set up,
operated by judges of little background who used an
old statute against witchcraft to convict many persons
without sufficient legal evidence. More women were accused. Confession meant escaping death. But as always
there were persons who rose above the ordinary and

refused to admit to that which they knew was not true. Giles Corey, rather than lie, was pressed to death by having weights piled on his body. Sarah Good, arrested with Tituba, told the judge that she was not a witch "and if you take away my life, God will give you blood to drink." Sarah was executed. The judge died soon after, his mouth overflowing with blood from what would seem to have been a cerebral hemorrhage.

Eventually, the pendulum swung back and saner minds grappled with the situation. More and more people began to see that the witch-hunt had gotten out of hand. Within a few months, Samuel Parris was voted out of his church by his parishioners, many of whom were as guilty as he was. By May 1693 the governor had released from jail everyone accused of witchcraft. Five years later the jurors who had handed down the guilty verdicts publicly admitted they had been duped. These actions, however, could not restore the lives of twenty people who had been put to death for not confessing to a crime of which they were not guilty.

And what of the people who had fostered the movement? History does not tell what became of Abigail Williams or her friends. Did they marry and become respected members of the community? Their crimes were, after all, the fruits of immature minds. This cannot be said of the adults. In the case of the older leaders, justice did triumph. The power play of the Puritan hierarchy was a death blow to its control over Salem.

The only contribution that can be credited to this shameful episode in American history is its addition to the English language of the term "witch-hunt," defined in the Thorndike-Barnhart Dictionary as "persecuting or defaming [a person] to gain a political advantage."

The Salem witch-hunt might be labeled the first unofficial example of vigilantism in America. Yet the connection to the neo-vigilantes of today is strong. For one thing, the danger was purely psychological. No one in Salem was harmed by witches. Actually, no one was guilty, because there were no witches. Those who claimed they had been subjected to injury were liars. The same question of guilt could be raised concerning the homosexuals in Queens as well as Professor Bohmer in San Diego. Did the homosexuals commit a crime against anyone, or was their threat merely in the minds of the residents, too? Did Professor Bohmer poison the minds of his college students, or was the fear of the San Diego right-wingers so great that they imagined his teaching to be evil?

The matter of injustice exists in all three incidents. Twenty innocent people died in Salem. A number of individuals were driven from a park area in Queens to which they had legal access. In addition bystanders who were angered by the illegal destruction of public property were threatened. In San Diego an innocent girl was shot by vigilantes.

If Salem was an unofficial incident of vigilantism then there is an official beginning. "The South Carolina Regulators of 1767 constituted America's first vigilante movement," wrote Richard Maxwell Brown in *Violence in America*. Also, the elements of the South Carolina situation correspond more closely to the picture that forms in the average person's mind when he or she encounters the term "vigilante."

Settlement of the back country of South Carolina began during the 1730s. This area stretched from about fifty miles inland to the Piedmont plateau. By 1758 the population numbered around twenty thousand people, mostly whites. Agriculture provided their livelihood.

An uneasy truce had existed between the farmers and the Cherokee Indians to the northwest. The peace was soon ended by whites who broke the treaties and by the militant Indian braves who influenced tribal decisions. Sporadic Indian attacks against farms in the pine forests started and then escalated into full-fledged war. The Cherokees burned houses and butchered the settlers' cattle. Farmers were scalped; their families were taken prisoner or dispersed. Hundreds of families abandoned their plantations and gathered in forts for protection. They were joined by the orphaned and homeless. These pockets of safety quickly became overcrowded, and food and clothing became scarce.

Savagery was not confined to the Indian warriors. Whites, too, butchered Indians, scalping them or cutting their bodies into pieces, which were fed to dogs. Fort commanders stole precious supplies sent to the homeless who were under the forts' protection. The army of Rangers, who were supposed to help the settlers, plundered isolated settlements and in some cases inflicted more harm than the Indians.

The Indians were driven back into the mountains in 1761. A treaty was signed that ended the war, but the desolation left behind was great. Plantations lay vacant and uncultivated. Few crops had been planted and even less were harvested. Livestock had been stolen or else had run wild. And, worse, the entire social structure was tottering.

The only form of local government in the back country was that composed of justices of peace, constables, and the militia. The justices of the peace, appointed by the governor in Charleston, could fine people up to twenty pounds in civil cases, but their powers did not extend to criminal affairs. The constables were similar to court officers who carried out the rulings of the justices of the peace. The back-country militia totaled 6,500 men. Their efficiency was at its best in military-type operations and was least effective when dealing with day-to-day civic affairs. So the back country, which was about a week's horseback ride from Charleston, virtually had no government. The people wanted a system of law and order, but their demands could not be met by the colonial leaders in Charleston.

The back country's population had grown by the middle 1760s to about thirty-five thousand persons. The area was rural, with small farms, averaging two hundred acres, on which were raised grain, tobacco, flax, and madder, the root of which was used to make a red dye. The small planter could not afford to buy laborers in the Charleston slave markets, so he and his family did all the work. Consequently, the average back countryman had a low regard for those who did not work as hard as he did.

The area leaders were those small farmers who, through hard work or cleverness or both, had acquired larger landholdings that produced the profitable crops of indigo, hemp, or wheat. Storekeepers and other businessmen sometimes gained admittance to the higher echelon, too. The smaller landowners admired these successful men and, though they all came from the same stock, put great emphasis on the word of the leading men.

The third social level was what Richard Maxwell Brown called "lower people" in *The South Carolina Regulators*. This group was made up of "Crackers" or ruffians and planters who had failed or whose holdings had been wiped out by the war with the Cherokee Indians. Other members were debtors, gamblers, squatters, and hunters. The people of this social level never formed an organized crime unit, but they were known to engage in squatting, poaching, or sneak thievery. Some, however, did drift into the several outlaw gangs that also inhabited the back country. These gangs were headed by war veterans who were unwilling or psychologically unable to return to peacetime normalcy or by men who had deserted honest living for the more lucrative earnings of crime. Many persons who had been orphaned or made homeless by the Cherokee War swelled the ranks of the banditti.

So the back country of South Carolina entered the middle 1760s with unsettled economic problems, a splintered society, and worst of all, practically no stabilizing government. The future was predictable, because violence is usually the visible manifestation of turbulent social conditions.

Attacks by the outlaw gang slowly grew in intensity until a wave of terror gripped the Carolinian hills. The bandits lived in communities with their wives and children. When the female population dwindled, the outlaws sacked plantations and farms, carrying off girls and women. Farmers were tortured until they revealed the whereabouts of hidden money. They were then robbed. The *South Carolina and American General Gazette* reported in August 1767 that anyone . . .

> . . . who had honestly earned as much as £50 and put it away for the future thereby jeopardized his own life. No man was safe who was rumored to have such a sum.

Not only money was taken. Livestock was slaughtered or stolen. South Carolina even had a way station that was part of an intercolonial network of horse thieves.

The respectable landowners were forced to turn their homes into veritable armed castles. Desperately, they pleaded for help from the Charleston authorities. The back-country settlers wanted protection and firm justice. But when six bandits were convicted in court, Governor Montague pardoned five. He had recently been elected and wanted to begin his term with acts of clemency.

The untenable state of affairs fit a prerequisite for the formation of vigilantes that has existed from then until the present day: if recognized authorities seem unwilling or unable to handle a problem, citizens then unite to find a solution.

Gangs of outraged settlers in the back country decided to supply the missing law. They formed loosely organized mobs and retaliated by attacking bandit settlements, burning them and then flogging and scattering the inhabitants. When the governor ordered these settler mobs to end their illegal activities, the vigilantes responded by organizing into a more formal unit. One thousand men were chosen and assumed the name Regulators. The members included the beleaguered small planters as well as the leaders of the back country. The person's standing socially affected his position of authority in the Regulators. Invariably, the leaders were the outstanding men of the area.

Conciliatory meetings between the governor and the Regulators resulted in the governor sending additional Ranger companies into the back country. Ironically, the captains of some of the Ranger units had been (or were) members of the Regulators. So, in effect, the governor had merely legalized the vigilantes. Some people even referred to the troops as Regulators rather than Rangers.

The Rangers-Regulators were very effective in eliminating crime. More bandit settlements were attacked. Horse thieves were tracked down and executed on the spot. The Charleston courtrooms filled with men apprehended by the Rangers-Regulators. Gangs of outlaws fled the back country. Outbreaks of crime lessened and then ceased. Their work done, the Rangers returned to official duty in the coastal region.

With the overt criminals removed, the Regulators now turned their attention to the so-called "lower people." The industrious, straight-living farmers disliked the presence of the indolent and immoral as much as they had disliked the outlaws. Since South Carolina had no vagrancy law, the Regulators issued their own. Anyone the vigilantes felt was not a decent, hard-working individual could expect a visit from the Regulators. The accused was subjected to fifty lashes and then sent to a plantation where he or she was used as a slave laborer. Freedom only came when the vigilantes felt the prisoner had been rehabilitated.

All this was done without the supervision of impartial judges. No legal evidence was presented, so there were no barriers to prevent the actions of the vigilantes from reflecting the personal grudges of some of the vigilante leaders. The situation roughly resembles the Queens, New York, problem related earlier, where the residents felt the homosexuals did not measure up to the community's moral code. In Queens the punishment was exile; in South Carolina a merciless whipping and then a slave labor camp.

Justice, however, caught up with the Regulators. Victims of their cruel and illegal punishments appeared in the Charleston provincial court. Some Regulators were found guilty and fined. Fearing further punishment, the Regulators defied the Charleston authorities by not recognizing the court-issued writs. Several process servers were abused when they ventured into the back country. The governor sent small bands of militia to subdue the Regulators. Battles ensued. Captured militiamen were whipped and sent packing. The colony was on the brink of full-scale rebellion.

Governor Montague was in Philadelphia so Lieutenant-Governor Bull held the governmental reins in the colony. He issued two proclamations. On August 3, 1768, he demanded the suppression of the Regulators, noting their illegal whippings and imprisonment of the lower people as well as the defiance of court processes. Three days later he offered pardon to all who would keep the peace from that point on. The first proclamation was mostly ignored by the back-country justices, who feared vigilante reprisals. So through a lack of enforcement and the pardoning of the Regulators, the leaders in Charleston had virtually accepted Regulator rule of the back country.

Outside events also affected the government's attempt to deal with the vigilantes. The Regulators turned their efforts from illegal processes to electing Regulator members to the assembly. This was a step which, if it had succeeded, might have transformed the Regulators from a vigilante group into a legal one that would follow the laws because the members would have a voice in framing the laws.

Meanwhile, however, England had passed the Townshend Acts that imposed import levies on glass, lead, paints, paper, and tea on the American colonists. An angry Massachusetts assembly wrote to all the colonies, asking that they oppose these new taxes. When the recently elected South Carolina assembly (which now contained Regulators) endorsed the Massachusetts letter, Governor Montague dissolved the assembly.

Thus by midwinter 1768 the avenue toward legalized law and order had closed. The Regulators remained in complete control of the back country. Their activities had risen one more step. Now their influence extended into most areas of daily life: supervising morals and family life, collecting debts, and trying to solve the labor shortage. The last was already being accomplished by the vagrancy law.

The total power of the Regulators was not accepted with equal happiness by all inhabitants of the back country. There were those who had personal feuds with Regulators. The lower people were angered by the treatment they received. Others were frightened by a volunteer group usurping complete governmental powers without authorization. Lastly, those average citizens who had first been pleased when the Regulators attacked the crime problem now, like the residents of Salem, were disgusted by the sadistic punishments meted out by the Regulators.

John Harvey who lived on Nobles Creek was found to have a horse that did not belong to him. One day fifty or sixty Regulators took Harvey prisoner and, binding him to a small tree, began beating him with small bundles of rods and switches. Fiddles played and drums beat gaily while each of the Regulators took his turn administering ten strokes. Bystanders were invited to join in the festivities. Many declined, too horrified by the blood that streamed down Harvey's back and by the glee of his tormentors. Others took part in the whipping, knowing little or nothing about the man's crime or if indeed he was guilty of any crime.

Word about this sort of treatment suffered by men at the hands of Regulators spread throughout the back country. A countergroup called the Moderators was formed. The Moderators' tactics strikingly resembled those they had vowed to fight. They seized whatever supplies they needed from inhabitants, and shot or beat the people who came to their camps to protest the thefts.

One Saturday in March 1769 some six to seven hundred Regulators assembled near a likesized group of Moderators. Guns were loaded and plans laid for an all-out battle. Fortunately, three men who were well respected by both sides arrived and were able to convince everyone to agree to a truce. The March 25, 1769, agreement between the Regulators and the Moderators was the end of the vigilante movement. A few isolated bands refused to break up, but with the passage of the Circuit Court Act in November of that year, courts, sheriffs, and duly-appointed officials became the colony's legally constituted law-enforcement body.

"An American tradition had begun," wrote Richard Maxwell Brown in *Violence in America,* "for as the pioneers moved across the Appalachian Mountains, the regulator-vigilante impulse followed the sweep of settlers toward the Pacific. The model for dealing with frontier disorder provided by the South Carolina Regulators was utilized over and over by American settlers."

2

The Threat of Frontier Living

Vigilantism in the Old West

Vigilantism came west to the plains, the Rockies, and the Pacific coast, playing a dominant role in an era that was rough, boisterous, and wild. The western-frontier form of vigilantism is perhaps the most widely known and, in many cases, considered to be a highly honored tradition in American history. Situations involving vigilantism have been romanticized as well as depicted tragically in literature, on stage, in music, and on film. Some versions are true; most are false.

First, a look at the conditions that fomented this hectic period of do-it-yourself justice. Vigilantism arises from the people, and the persons who streamed westward during the 1800s were a special lot. The Revolution, the Mexican War, and the War Between the States produced men and women who had faced death and had survived. Many of them were not content to return to their old settled and static lives. By conquering hardships they had developed a supreme confidence in their ability to surmount the rigors of a new life on the frontier.

Other persons left their homes to seek instant wealth or to be their own masters. They were willing to risk the almost-certain dangers for a life that, as of yet, had no boundaries. Another group was the losers: persons determined to begin anew and this time to succeed. And, last, there were the dishonest. The newly opened lands were virgin territory; the criminals knew conditions would be disorganized and that the stabilizing elements of society—church and government—would be weak.

The men and women who went West did so with a reason strong enough to make them ready to tackle the odds. As a result, a certain frontier philosophy took shape. The people were extremely self-reliant and independent. "Decision was made on the spot, face to face. The questions were simple, the solutions, equally simple," wrote Richard Maxwell Brown. The deliberative individual was scorned. Life was too dangerous for a person to take a long time to decide what was to be done In many cases he who hesitated was truly lost.

Settlements sprang up overnight. The people who had borne the burdens of the trip usually worked well together. Everyone *had* to cooperate; the enemy was the environment, and it was all around them. Families lived in tents or sod houses until they could construct more substantial buildings. People's possessions consisted only of what was truly necessary, but they had to be light enough to be brought with them, as well. Only the practical pieces survived. Objects of great sentimental value or that might have meant a bit more comfort were strewn along wagon train trails from Pennsylvania to the Rockies.

So property was highly valued not only because people had so little, but the loss of a man's horse or cattle might mean death for him and his family. Not until life began to run with a reasonable smoothness did people think about law enforcement. By that time it was often too late.

Frontier existence was hard for the honest and the circumstances encouraged crime. Banks required weeks and often months to be organized so federal paper money was scarce. The need was filled by private bank notes. The times became America's notorious age of counterfeiting. Horses, in certain instances, were used as barter as well as transportation or beasts of burden. Open ranges aided horse thieves. Sometimes the printing of fake money and the stealing of horses were linked. Both types of criminals operate best by commiting their crime in one spot and then moving quickly to another spot hundreds of miles away.

The few law-enforcement officials in the West had a mammoth job to do. In 1877 Texas alone had five thousand men on the wanted list. Fugitives took to the back country where pursuit was almost impossible. Should a criminal be captured, the next problem was where to put him. If there was a jail, the building was usually flimsy, and the jailed man's accomplices soon had him free. Territorial courts visited remote places sporadically, sometimes only two or at most four times a year. Local courts were notoriously corrupt. Outlaws bribed and intimidated juries or witnesses or judges. At times all three were influenced by the lawbreakers. When the due processes of law were observed, the pace was too slow and the punishment too lenient to suit pioneer temperament. People back in the nineteenth century, like some people in the 1970s, often claimed that the American legal system favored the guilty rather than the victim.

The social upheaval of the frontier period produced lawlessness in every state. When the citizens attempted to control the crime rate, a counterwave of their "mobocracy" resulted. These irate-citizen mobs usually adopted the original name of Regulators, but others called themselves Slickers, Stranglers, Committees of Safety, or Vigilance Committees. The last produced the shortened term "vigilante" and the name for the system: *vigilantism*.

In the 1970s there are those who cry for a return to "the good-old-fashioned justice" of the West. How many of these advocates would be willing to face such mobs? They would probably argue that they would not have to be judged by a jury of vigilantes because they were not guilty. The idea that all those punished by vigilantes were guilty is only one of the misconceptions about the vigilante system of justice.

The belief that citizen justice arose to fill the void of legal law enforcement is another misconception about frontier vigilantism, although there were remote circumstances in which it was true that it did. One such case concerns the tragic circumstances of the Donner Party's dangerous trip from Missouri to California in 1846–47.

From the outset the wagon train was beset with trouble. Though the emigrants had left early enough to be able to avoid the snow, they lost their way and it was a month before they reached Great Salt Lake. In the salty swamps southwest of the lake, they encountered more difficulties, causing further delays. The time of the snow was nearly upon them. Tempers were raw; panic had begun to tighten its grip. If the wagon train did not make up the lost time, disaster awaited them in the mountains.

One day John Snyder began whipping another man's team to drive the horses faster. The owner, James Reed, objected. Snyder swung around and flailed the man. Incensed, Reed pulled a knife. Reed's wife ran between the two men to prevent a fight and was struck by the whip. Reed, blood streaming into his eyes, stabbed and killed Snyder.

Justice now was the problem. Missouri lay several months behind the wagon train. The killing occurred at Gravelly Ford. The place was within the Mexican territory, but far beyond the jurisdiction of any Mexican officials. There seemed only one answer. The respected members of the wagon train met as a court.

Reed defended himself by saying he was protecting his wife. And in that violent, emotional moment he had attacked Snyder who still clutched the whip. To show his remorse, Reed had used boards from his own wagon to construct Snyder's rough coffin. Today that may seem inconsequential, but in those times a person's wagon was the sole means by which he or she could reach the destination. The wagons were truly models of economical and practical construction: the wagon body was as light as possible and every board had a use. If a wagon failed, the family often had to be left behind because every bit of available space in the other wagons was filled. So by weakening his wagon's structure Reed had, in effect, lessened his own chances of conquering the towering Sierras.

Today, a court studying Reed's case would take into consideration the debilitating effects of the journey as well as the circumstances of the moment. The verdict would probably be justifiable homicide. Not so with the Donner jury. Possibly they convicted Reed in hopes of quelling more outbreaks. At any rate, though the verdict was unfavorable, the men did not want to execute Reed. Instead they banished him, unarmed, from the train. By doing so they must have realized they were virtually condemning him to death, as the desolate territory was ridden with hostile Indians. That night, however, Reed's daughter smuggled a gun and ammunition to him.

James Reed reached California safely, but the Donner Party became snowbound in a high Sierra pass. Many members died of starvation while some who survived did so by resorting to cannibalism. James Reed was one of the persons in the rescue party that saved the remnants of the Donner Party.

Here then was an instance in which there was no governmental agency to fall back on. The conditions were similar to those of life aboard the sailing ships of the time that gave the captain full authority to deal with criminals. But many times a regular court was available if the vigilantes had been willing to wait the proper amount of time.

In 1850 the delay in the trial of a man named Jim would have been from night to the following morning. However, the Sacramento, California, vigilantes preferred their justice swift. An account of the episode is given by Henry J. Coke in *A Ride Over the Rocky Mountains to Oregon and California.* The author arrived on the scene shortly after the incident's culmination, and thus learned the details in retrospect.

The story actually began at a gold digging called Cigar Bar. One day a man named Jim arrived and started his own search for the precious metal. "Jim was a Britisher," said a man from Sacramento. "That is, he come from a place they call Botany Bay [Australia], which belongs to [Queen] Victoria, but ain't exactly in the old country." The story teller worked alongside Jim at Cigar Bar.

Within two weeks a man lost about three hundred dollars he had stashed away. "Somehow suspicions fell on Jim." But before he could be confronted about the crime, Jim followed his friend's advice and fled. Six months later the man who had so kindly counseled Jim to leave the diggings, came upon him in a Sacramento gambling hall. "And all day and night Jim used to play at faro, and roulette, and a heap of other games. Nobody couldn't tell how he made his money last so long." A blacksmith decided he had found the answer. One night a quarrel broke out when the blacksmith accused Jim of cheating. The blacksmith struck Jim on the mouth. "Jim jumped from his seat, pulled a revolver from his pocket, and shot the blacksmith dead on the spot." Jim's friendly adviser was the first to grab hold of the Australian.

Though Judge Parker held court in Sacramento, a

trial was conducted in the gambling parlor. Guilt was
not the question during the two-hour trial. The debate
ranged over the question whether to wait for the Criminal Court to meet the next day or hang Jim by "Lynch
Law," the unwritten code which favored hanging guilty
people without a legal trial. "The best speakers said that
Lynch Law was no law, and endangered the life of every
innocent man: but the mob would have it that he was to
die at once."

The mob ruled.

At daybreak the next morning—mere hours before
the legal court would have convened—Jim was carried
to the horse market where a huge elm tree grew. As the
rope was about to be placed around his neck, Jim
grabbed the cord and swung himself onto a branch above
the crowd's reach. He knotted the rope himself and
slipped it over his head. Then he spoke to the people below.

"He didn't say much, except that he hated them all.
He cursed the man he shot; he then cursed the world;
and last of all, he cursed himself."

And with that, he leaped from the branch.

Would Judge Parker's court have convicted Jim? In
all probability Jim's life would have ended by hanging.
This episode does not illustrate how innocent men die
by vigilante action, but rather it demonstrates that
vigilantism is infectious. Once men are accustomed to
taking the law into their own hands, they continue to do
so even when appropriate steps might be followed.

Looking back over the facts of Jim's case, the way that
suspicion first centered on him indicates another mis-

nomer about vigilante justice. It is not justice at all.
"Somehow suspicions fell on Jim," said the man who had
known Jim in the goldfields. The reason might have
been that Jim was Australian. Although all nationalities
and races worked the digs, those who were not native
Americans came under suspicion the fastest. Vigilante
mobs were and are notoriously prejudiced.

When violence erupted in the frontier, the conflict was
often between reds and whites. "The only good Indian
is a dead Indian," was a popular saying and belief of the
times. Blacks were not able to rise above a worker level.
Orientals were targets for potshots without any fear that
the trigger puller would be prosecuted. In parts of the
South lynching a Negro was legal just as shooting an
Indian or beating an Oriental or Mexican was socially
and legally permissible in other parts of the country.
Vigilantism worked against the lowly, the unpopular,
those least able to fend off attacks. Californian vigilantes
dealt more severe penalties to Mexicans, Chinese, and
Chileans than to other captives. Too often vigilantism
was merely a means for persecuting a minority rather
than restoring law and order.

The biggest defense of frontier vigilantism was the
claim that the vigilantes' courts were more efficient. This
could well be true, especially if efficient means swift. It
is far from true if efficient means free from error.

Many precepts of our law have come down from the
Babylonian Code of Hammurabi and, for good reason,
have remained an integral part of our legal juris-
prudence. The concepts are designed to protect an innocent person from being judged guilty. When a suspect

is apprehended, the individual is acquainted with his or her rights so that he or she will not make incriminating statements through fear. The person is then considered innocent until proven guilty in the courtroom. The judge who sits over the court is impartial and is there to be certain that the proceedings run according to law. The judge sees that the defendant is not harassed. The jury that decides the accused's fate is composed of that person's peers, and the members are chosen for their fairness. The penalty imposed, if the verdict is guilty, is commensurate with the crime and aimed toward making the defendant a better citizen. The whole process is slow, methodical, and designed to prevent, as much as humanly possible, a miscarriage of justice.

Vigilante courts bypassed all these basic tenets. Anyone confronted with a frontier mob was considered guilty. Vigilantes, past and present, always believe they are completely in the right. Torture was often used to extract a confession. Impartiality at a vigilante court was a joke. The judge and jury were chosen from the vigilante band who already firmly believed in the accused person's guilt. Often the defendant was not allowed to bring anyone to testify in his or her behalf. Even if such testimony were permitted, who would dare antagonize the vigilante mob by speaking out against the mob's intentions? Such a courageous individual might be the next victim. The penalties imposed by the court were final with no attempt at rehabilitation.

In *The History of Denver* W. N. Byers, an old Denver, Colorado, vigilante of 1860, remembered:

We never hanged on circumstantial evidence. I have known a great many such executions, but I don't believe one of them was ever unjust. But when they were proven guilty, they were always hanged. There was no getting out of it. No, there were no appeals in those days; no writs of errors, no attorneys' fees; no pardon in six months. Punishment was swift, sure and certain.

"Swift" could well describe the whole concept of frontier vigilantism. It is not the adjective that ought to be applied in describing a well-devised court system. The legal code is there so that citizens have protection from the guilty and the guiltless are not wrongly judged.

The frontier tradition helped form many traits of modern America. The era fostered individuality like no other in history. The democratic belief that all persons are equal was, for the most part, put into action in western settlements. Though there were exceptions, for the first time people achieved social, economic, and political mobility. Paupers became gold or copper kings, wielding tremendous political influence. The whole period was marked by material progress and gave drive to the national spirit that still influences the nation in the 1970s.

Rightfully, Americans take pride in their frontier heritage. But this feeling should not blind the people to the fact that many of the American institutions originated under harsh conditions. And some of them, like vigilantism, prove to be faulty when examined more objectively.

3

The Fruit of Economic Change

The San Francisco
Committees of Vigilance

San Francisco is one of the unique cities of the world. Even the most reluctant Americans admit that if they had to reside in an urban area, "It would be San Francisco." For each person the reasons differ. The charisma of modern San Francisco might depend on the hills, the sea, the fog, the street-corner flower stalls, or the sense of history. Whatever it is, San Francisco captivates hearts like few other cities in the world. San Francisco also has a past filled with more lawlessness, blood spilling, and vigilantism than most other cities. But that was a few steps up the ladder of time.

First came the Indians, settling on the high, white cliffs and sand hills as well as fishing in the ocean, bay, or nearby rivers. In 1579 Sir Francis Drake may or may not have landed on the shore of what is now Drake's Bay just outside the Golden Gate strait. Some researchers believe Drake touched Californian soil farther up the coast and missed the Golden Gate because of heavy fog. At any rate, the English became interested in the area as did the Russians. The Spanish moved the fastest, however, and soon set up Mission Dolores in order to convert the Indians to Christianity. In March 1848 a school commission totaled the population of San Francisco at eight hundred and twelve people.

Meanwhile, on January 24, 1848, James W. Marshall scooped some shiny yellow pebbles from a newly dug channel on the south fork of the American river. He dropped them into the dented crown of his hat and continued inspecting the sawmill that John Sutter had hired him to build. Later, when Marshall reported the structure's progress to his boss, he and Sutter assayed the yellow metal. Few test results have had such a shattering impact as those reached at Sutter's Fort. The Gold Rush was on!

The nearest seaport to Sutter's mill was San Francisco where the cliff-ribbed strait protected a bay which ran fifty miles from north to south and fourteen miles in an easterly direction. San Francisco became the point of disembarkation for fortune hunters arriving by sea. By the end of 1849 the population had reached twenty-five thousand, an increase of almost 3,000 per cent in twenty-one months. The city slowly climbed the sand hills. First there were tents, adobe houses, and flimsy wooden shacks. Later wooden buildings replaced the makeshift structures, and then came brick. The streets, mudholes in wet weather and dust bowls in hot, dry periods, were lined with saloons, gambling halls, and boarding houses.

More people arrived daily on ships from many countries. The largest national group was the Chinese. Not far behind them numerically were the Irish, the Germans, and the British. Half the population of San Francisco was foreign-born. Persons with dreams of instant wealth walked down the gangplanks to find rough competition and raw conditions. Most males carried a gun or bowie knife, for the streets of San Francisco were only slightly less hazardous than the Sierra goldfields. Crime conditions were so severe that newspapers called for a popular uprising to quell the crime rate.

At the base of Telegraph Hill was Sydney Town. The tents and hovels were filled with Australian convicts who either had been allowed to leave their jails or had escaped on sailing ships. The "Ducks" or "Coves" as the Australians were labeled, roamed the unlighted city streets, robbing at will. Yet Sydney Town was not the greatest source of crime.

A large canvas structure on Kearney Street called Tammany Hall housed the Hounds, or San Francisco Society of Regulators. The Hounds were ex-New York Volunteers, deserters as well as men who had been discharged at the end of the Mexican War. They had lingered in San Francisco and were that city's largest single group of lawbreakers. The one hundred or so ruffians wore their old army clothes, raided saloons and stores and stole and destroyed anything of value. They were so fierce that they were often employed by peace officers to make arrests or collect debts.

In July 1849 the Hounds visited Chileno Village, or Little Chile, to collect a five hundred dollar debt. The term "Chilean" in old California referred to anyone from South or Latin America. Most of the Chileans were away from their settlement possibly having been warned about the hoodlums' approach. The Hounds ransacked the area, beating any Chileans they encountered. Some men raped a young girl and murdered her mother when the woman tried to protect her daughter. The tents and shacks were set ablaze. Triumphantly, the Hounds returned to Tammany Hall to tally up their loot.

The next morning a thirty-six-year-old ex-Mainer, Sam Brannan, mounted a barrel on the corner of Clay and Montgomery Streets only blocks away from Tammany Hall. He described to passersby the shameful deeds of the previous night, entreating them to help his campaign to make San Francisco a safer city. Two hundred and thirty citizens enrolled in a vigilante gang. By evening seventeen Hounds had been arrested and incarcerated on the U.S.S. "Warren." The ship's brig was considered the one jail where other Hounds would be unable to liberate their companions. Samuel Roberts, the unofficial leader of the Hounds, tried to escape by hiding behind sacks of flour on a vessel heading upriver to Stockton. His attempt failed. The vigilantes, unlike many similar groups, did not enact their own justice. Instead, they delivered the now twenty captives, including Roberts, to a legitimate court.

Two defense attorneys and, at the last moment, a prosecutor stepped forward to take part in the trial. Only nine Hounds were convicted. There was strong suspicion at the time that much of the testimony given in behalf of the Hounds was perjured. The court's

verdict was respected, however, which was another unusual facet of this particular incidence of vigilantism. No
extralegal attempt was made to punish all twenty apprehended men. Samuel Roberts was sentenced to ten
years' imprisonment while the other eight received lesser
terms. Another question now had to be answered. California had no penitentiary and the Navy would not im-
prison the men for a lengthy duration. The solution was
to exile the guilty, promising the men death by lynching
if they ever returned to San Francisco. At the conclusion
of the trial this first San Franciscan vigilante group disbanded, once again being the exception to the rule.

Still the gold seekers poured into San Francisco. On
Christmas Eve 1849 a fire broke out that leveled a large
portion of the growing city. The various nationalities
became part of the new business section that rose from
the ashes of the old. French, Chinese, Italian, and
Spanish restaurants did a lively business. Chinese laun-
dries opened up in most sections of the city. In 1850
California was admitted to the Union. The same year
three more fires caused widespread damage to San
Francisco. Many citizens suspected the fires were being
set as a cover for robbery and looting. A fifth conflagra-
tion flared on May 4, 1851. The merchants and me-
chanics formed patrols, hoping to prevent further crime.
On June 2 an arsonist was caught in the act. This time
the blaze was quickly contained.

Now the merchants decided there was need for a
larger and more effective group of guards, and they asked
Sam Brannan, the veteran leader of the first vigilante
band that had acted against the Hounds, to head the

Committee of Vigilance of 1851, which came to be known as the Committee. Two hundred men signed up. The group's first victim was John Jenkins who was caught rowing away from Long Wharf with a safe that did not belong to him. This time the Committee did not follow the prescribed legal procedure. Possibly finding suitable jail space was still a problem, or perhaps the Committee recalled the fixed trial of the Hounds. At any rate, by midnight they themselves had tried Jenkins and found him guilty. At two o'clock the following morning, Jenkins was hanged.

For the next three months the Committee assiduously went about cleaning up San Francisco, receiving staunch support from the more affluent citizens and, especially, the newspapers. Not everyone believed in the anticrime methods, however. Governor John McDougal opposed the Committee's activities. Subsequently, he suffered a loss in popularity because of his outspoken stand and was not returned to office.

The vigilantes of 1851 set an impressive record. Ninety-one men were seized. Though the Committee for the most part conducted its own trials, the vigilantes did not subscribe to the usual mob precept that all those apprehended were automatically guilty. The San Francisco vigilantes convicted only a portion of those arrested. Four men were hanged and twenty-eight were banished from the city. More lenient punishments were inflicted upon sixteen others. Forty-one men were freed. The psychological effect of the group, however, was even more sweeping. Hundreds of criminals fled the area.

Despite the organization's success, three influences

brought about its demise. One was the sharp drop in crime which was directly attributable to the vigilantes' presence. Conditions stabilized enough that the Committee felt times were safe for law enforcement to be returned to the proper authorities. Another reason was the Committee's growing unpopularity. The bench and bar as well as church groups launched strong attacks against the inequities of justice they felt existed in vigilante courts. The third reason the Committee of Vigilance of 1851 ceased operating was that many of its members were businessmen whose main interest was making money, not preventing crime. No end date can be given for the group. The last entry in the Committee journal was written on June 30, 1851.

The crime rate of California and particularly of San Francisco did not go into a permanent slump, however. With the fade-out of the Vigilance Committee, there was a gradual reemergence of criminal activity. By the fall of 1855, San Francisco was once again the scoundrel's paradise the city had been before June 1851. Newspapers renewed their call for a revival of citizen justice, citing the one thousand murders that had taken place between 1849 and 1856. The regular court system had convicted only one murderer in the same period.

As usual a catalyst was needed to initiate the birth of a vigilante mob. The ingredient in this instance was a man who called himself James King of William and who had migrated to San Francisco from Georgetown, at the time a sleepy suburb of Washington, D.C. James King of William had been simply James King at first, but because another James King had also lived in

Georgetown and there was constant confusion over the similar names, he had tacked his father's given name to his own.

In Washington, King had worked for Riggs and Corcoran, a banking firm, but had lost his health. The usual cure prescribed at the time was travel, and King went to Peru, Chile, and finally ended his journey in San Francisco. Entering into banking for a second time, he failed dismally. Journalism seemed a good possibility for bringing in an income sufficient to support his wife and small children. On October 8, 1855, the first issue of his *Daily Evening Bulletin* slid from the printing press.

The *Bulletin* was a one-man paper. Publishing a newspaper at this stage in the development of the printed media certainly seemed a wise decision for King. The era of the individualistic, crusading newspaper editor was dawning. Eight years later William Randolph Hearst was born on Nob Hill in King's adopted city and halfway across the country Joseph Pulitzer would be landing his first newspaper job on a St. Louis German-language publication. The fearless, blistering editorials written by King might have fitted right in with the products of these future ink-and-newsprint giants.

Less than six weeks after King had started his newspaper, an unarmed U.S. Marshall was gunned down by a gambler named Charles Cora. When the case came to court, Cora's lawyer managed to get a hung jury. For the next few weeks Cora waited in his cell, knowing as most people did in San Francisco that his release was only a matter of time. Nightly, crowds gathered outside the jail demanding Cora's death. King rallied behind the people, adding the *Bulletin*'s voice to the loud demands for an appropriate punishment. King's popularity and the *Bulletin*'s circulation grew.

While this fight was going on, King initiated another campaign in his newspaper. James P. Casey was a city supervisor who had the distinction of having supposedly invented a ballot box that was extremely easy to stuff. The *Bulletin* charged Casey with laxity and rigged elections. In one editorial, King revealed that Casey was a former inmate of New York State's Sing Sing Prison. When Casey arrived at the *Bulletin*'s offices, King refused to see him and had the man escorted from the premises.

That night Casey hid behind an express wagon parked along King's homeward route. As the fiery editor trudged past, Casey stepped out and shot King. The seriously wounded man was carried into a nearby Pacific Express office and a doctor was summoned. The prognosis: James King of William was too badly wounded to live. Casey, meanwhile, had fled through dark streets to the local jail where he knew he would be safe from the angry mob that had collected at the shooting scene. He was locked in a cell near another James King hater, Charles Cora.

At last the San Franciscan citizens who had been so distressed by social conditions had a nucleus around which to cluster. Some men asked William Tell Coleman, who had been a member of the Committee of Vigilance of 1851, to form a new vigilance committee. Coleman agreed, and by the following evening fifty-five hundred volunteers as well as strong financial backing had come forth, the latter provided by the wealthy citizens.

Fiction is a reflection of life. In 1856 San Francisco had a real-life situation with all the ingredients of exciting fiction: a martyr, an enemy, and an avenging force. And this is the way most history books depict the circumstances surrounding the formation of the Committee of Vigilance of 1856. A deeper look, however, is needed to fully understand the situation.

James King of William certainly would have been a formidable competitor of those publishing giants who thrived during the golden age of newspapers. King, like Hearst and Pulitzer, was aggressive and completely confident that he was in the right, and he utilized his newspaper to sway people. But, also like the other two men, King had his blind spots, his personal prejudices that determined the slant of many of his outbursts. King's pet hate was Catholicism. Not only were attacks waged against Charles Cora, an Italian-Catholic, and James P. Casey, an Irish-Catholic, but other anti-Romanist campaigns were conducted by the *Bulletin*. King's personal and editorial popularity was primarily due to the fact that many of the successful families of San Francisco were Protestant and strongly opposed the Irish-Catholic Democrats who controlled the city's political offices.

Cora and Casey personified the affluent citizens' pet hates. Though the two men were guilty of their respective crimes, the eagerness with which their punishment was sought probably stemmed as much from the citizenry's intolerance as from its desire for justice. Over-

powering muscle and monetary support were available
for the new vigilante band because people saw in the
vigilantes an opportunity to drag down the entrenched
Catholic politicians.

The Committee of 1856 did little to hide its prejudicial nature. From the outset blacks and Chinese were
not admitted to membership. Four days after King's
shooting, the vigilantes dragged a cannon to the jail-
house door and gave the authorities ten minutes to hand
over Casey and Cora. Several days later the two Catholics
appeared before a vigilante court. In the midst of the
testimony, the proceedings were halted for a dramatic
announcement: James King of William was dead. And
by dying, King probably got what he wanted most. The
emotion was so great in the ersatz court that Casey and
Cora were quickly declared guilty. On the day that a
bell was tolling for King's funeral, the two men were
hanged.

If cooler heads hoped this would end the vigilantism,
they were disappointed. Bolstered by success, the vigilantes set up an official headquarters. An old warehouse
on Clay Street was fortified and guarded by armed sen-
tries. Breastworks of earth-filled bags were placed around
the building. These sacks were to give the command post
its name: Fort Gunnybags. Writs of banishment issued
forth from Fort Gunnybags intended mostly for Irish
criminals.

As the activities and power of Fort Gunnybags gained
momentum, a countergroup, the Law and Order Committee, was organized. Some of the lawyers and state
officials who joined the new committee did so because

they had been refused admission to the vigilantes. Others, such as judges and former-Governor John Mc-Dougal, did so out of alarm. McDougal had been the governor who had vehemently opposed the earlier Committee of Vigilance.

In an effort to destroy the vigilantes, the Law and Order Committee requested arms from the governor. They were refused. Meanwhile four men had been hanged by the Committee of Vigilance, thirty more had been banished from the city, and approximately eight hundred criminals had fled to more hospitable regions. But public opposition was becoming increasingly evident. The state militia had plotted with the Law and Order Committee in an effort to thwart the Committee of Vigilance. The plan failed because informers for the Committee of Vigilance had infiltrated the ranks of the Law and Order band. But if the militia had failed once, they might try again. Knowing this, and feeling they had already done their job well, the Committee of Vigilance ripped down its fortifications. On August 18, 1856, close to six thousand members of the Committee staged a massive parade and were publicly and honorably dismissed from further duty. Fort Gunnybags was thrown open to a public reception. The Committee of 1856 had adjourned.

The San Francisco vigilantes are so well known that most people believe they were one of a kind. A mold had been cast, however, and other California cities followed San Francisco's example. In Monterey in 1864 and in Tulare ten years later, do-it-yourself justice erupted. The model was also used in the mining towns of Idaho, Montana, and Colorado. Even San Francisco had spurts of lesser vigilantism up to the beginning of the twentieth century. Actually San Francisco exemplified an era in American history: a time of explosive economic change. As the following chapters will show, the techniques used by the city's citizens to fight violence with violence have been employed time after time in other cities and areas throughout the United States.

What about a critical evaluation of the three major incidents of San Franciscan vigilantism? Certainly, history has been kind to them. The episodes are treated as instances of pioneer spirit, and the leaders and members are pictured as folk heroes. Usually no mention is made that the spirit intensified with each succeeding group. Or that each new outbreak gave the accused less leeway to be judged innocent and the vigilantes less self-awareness for error and fewer checks and balances that would assure the mob was not motivated by personal grudges.

Little remains in the San Francisco of today to remind people of the nineteenth-century lawlessness and unfair justice. A street called Brannan runs down to the Bay. Parallel to this byway named for the leader of the Committee of 1851 is King Street, which honors James King of William, the catalyst for the Committee of 1856. And high on a hill behind a small chapel is a cemetery of weatherworn stones. If the spokesman of the guided tour is not pressured by a tight schedule, he may explain that the chiseled phrase on these stones—"Killed by the V.C."—has nothing to do with the Viet Cong. Here lie some of the victims of the Vigilance Committee.

4

The Threat of Social Change

The Ku Klux Klan

Ironically, America—known as the Land of the Free—has a long and bloody history of vigilantism directed against racial and religious minorities.

In the days of the early settlers the United States awarded bounties to individuals who killed Indians. The bounty hunters, singly or in bands, murdered Indians, scalped them, and then turned the scalps over to U.S. authorities in exchange for money—so much per scalp. Eastern cities have seen anti-Irish riots; on the West Coast mobs of vigilantes have hunted down Mexican-Americans and Filipinos; first in the South, then later in various other U.S. areas, blacks have been the vigilantes' target.

One of the thousands of such vigilante groups whose activities have been aimed at minorities managed to become the most successful purveyor of hate in America's history. In Pulaski, Tennessee, just after the Civil War, six young men, all former college students and ex-military officers, decided to form a club. Their problem was idleness. Their purpose was to find something to do to entertain themselves. The men had a great time putting on funny disguises, riding all over town at night, and conducting a secret initiation filled with a college-fraternity type of hijinks.

From this boyish origin a vigilante organization was created that was to become a national phenomenon. The group would elect members to the U.S. Senate and to governors' mansions. These vigilantes were to hold national conventions and parade, over forty thousand-strong, down Pennsylvania Avenue in the nation's capital. A classic film praising their activities would be directed by one of the most famous men to emerge from the early days of Hollywood.

Thousands of people would be lynched, flogged, or tortured by members of this vigilante organization. Religious and racial divisions of all kinds would be inflamed. The mob's initials and symbol would come to be known by almost every American and be sufficiently powerful in themselves to terrorize people.

All this, because six young idlers formed a club that took its name from the Greek word for circle: *kuklos.* The word was divided and elongated, producing Ku Klux Klan. Many people mistakenly believe the Klan operated only in the South. At its peak, however, the KKK was widely accepted from California to New York State. The Klan's beginnings were Southern, though, and while it was getting a foothold during its early years,

it found comfort and support in the South. To understand the Ku Klux Klan it is necessary to understand
the South of 1865, the year the Klan was born in Pulaski, Tennessee.

The Civil War had ended in April of 1865, leaving
the area below the Mason-Dixon line in desperate straits.
The economy, which was basically rural and agricultural,
had been wrecked. Lands and crops had been destroyed.
The huge plantation system that had brought in the
cotton and tobacco income had depended upon slave
labor which was no longer available. The southerner
who would have to begin anew was demoralized, dis-
graced, and filled with hatred. The defeat in the war had
hurt a proud people. As a result, they despised north-
erners and blacks. The northerner had interfered with
their way of life, invaded their lands, and inflicted
northern philosophy on the South. The blacks who now
walked the street free men were considered inferior
beings. The proposition that they should have an equal
place in society was frightening to the southerner. Blacks
were a danger to the South and its symbol—the white
woman.

The status of the female was an integral part of the
southern culture. The chivalrous southern male had
placed her on a pedestal mainly because she marked in
his mind the ultimate division between blacks and
whites. She was inaccessible to blacks and therefore
represented the South which was held to be white territory with blacks relegated to a menial role. Any attack
on the South was an attack on the white woman. Any
attack on a white woman was an attack against the whole

southern concept. When the twentieth-century play-
wright, Tennessee Williams, wrote about the decaying
South, his main characters were southern women who
had fallen upon hard times.

In addition to a ravaged self-image and a wrecked
economy, the southern political picture was dismal.
With the war's end, President Andrew Johnson, following plans set forth by Lincoln, returned the reins of control to the white citizens. The postwar government
therefore had many former Confederate leaders who
even though they appeared to accept the new position of
the blacks only granted them limited status. Certainly,
access to the ballot box was something the white officials
would never entrust to the Negro. In some way, and
without resorting to open rebellion, a return to the
Old South had to be facilitated. Such were the conditions when six men conceived a fun-type group in
Pulaski, Tennessee.

Their nighttime rides that began for kicks produced
unexpected results. Blacks walking to their cabins at
night would hear the beat of a horse's hoofs. A ghostly
figure clad in white, flowing garments would draw to a
halt, staring down through dark slits. The ghoulish shape
would beg for water, saying he had not had a drink since
he died in the Battle of Shiloh. He had come up from
hell and had galloped around the world twice since
dinnertime. The viewers of this spectre were under-
standably upset. Blacks began remaining indoors at
night. It was then that the Ku Klux Klan tasted its potential power and found the flavor of fear to its liking.
Here was a means of controlling the blacks. No violence

was needed. No one would be harmed. And, certainly, no southern jury would convict a white for playing a little joke upon the blacks.

During the next two years word of the activities spread. New cells of the Ku Klux Klan were started. The offspring of the Pulaski Klan were self-contained units with only loose ties to the parent group. With so little outside discipline, overzealous members became more militant. Soon blacks were not only being frightened by the night riders but beaten or ordered from the county by sunrise. At this point the Klan was still a secret society, hidden by masks and using the cover of darkness for their forays. Political events, however, were to force it into a position of dominance in southern life.

During the Klan's formative years, discontent was spreading in the North over President Johnson's handling of the South's Reconstruction. People saw their onetime enemies back in power. The freedom given to blacks by the Fourteenth Amendment was not being granted. So Congress voted out the current methods and came up with a new formula. The lands that had been the Confederacy were divided into military districts. Existing governments were disbanded and new ones instituted. Leaders were drawn from the ranks of southern white antisecessionists or former northern military officers. With the arrival of new governments in 1867 and 1868, southern tempers boiled and the ranks of the Klan overflowed.

A meeting of the Klan representatives convened in Nashville, Tennessee, during April 1867. A constitution as well as lines of authority were drawn up. The stated goal of the Ku Klux Klan was to defend the weak, innocent, defenseless, and oppressed as well as the Constitution of the United States. The weak, innocent, defenseless, and oppressed referred to those southerners who were not allowed to follow their old prejudicial ways. The head of the Klan was given the title of Grand Wizard and his "Empire" was composed of realms, dominions, provinces, and dens. Subordinate leaders of these sections were Grand Dragons, Titans, Giants, and Cyclops. Members were appropriately called Ghouls.

"To the white Southerner, the Ku Klux Klan was a law-and-order movement because it was directed at the restoration of proper order," wrote David M. Chalmers in *Hooded Americanism*. Proper order, of course, meant proper *southern* order.

And the Klan did ride out to restore the old order. The means was violence. Klan members used threats, whips, knives, and hangmen's ropes. Anyone who did not support a return to ante-bellum traditions was a potential victim for the hooded vigilantes. Both whites and blacks were victims.

Yankee businessmen as well as Yankee politicians were driven from southern towns. Yankee teachers were a special target. Oppressors of all eras have realized that the road to freedom was paved by books and literature which inspire men's thinking. Before the Civil War, instructing a black in reading had been a serious crime. The southerners' perpetual fear—black insurrection—was lessened by the slaves' ignorance. With the advent of freedom and education for the former slaves, the southerner knew his control over the blacks was greatly weakened. The Klan burned many postwar schools. Teachers were tortured, murdered, or sent fleeing into the night, often without clothes on their backs. Other whites were attacked: judges and public officials who would not give the southern whites preferential treatment.

The blacks, however, were the prime recipients of Klan vengeance. Though liberty had been granted, blacks were still expected to follow the false, stereotyped image of a Negro: the shuffling, scraping, overly respectful individuals who "know their place" and by their very demeanor announce their acceptance of second-class-citizen status. Scare tactics were employed to frighten the blacks back into this position. Those who tried to raise their own level or the level of their race were kicked down again. Fearful fates awaited blacks who through self-initiative improved their farms or joined a political organization. In South Carolina the vigilantes attacked the black militia, flogging the militiamen and murdering the officers. Everywhere blacks were prevented from voting for the candidates of their choice. Either they were threatened into casting a ballot for the Conservative Party, which supported white supremacy, or terrorized into keeping away from the polls.

The campaign of fear and blood was so successful that internal and external troubles developed for the Klan during 1868. Any organization that is secret and composed of semi-autonomous sections is practically impossible to control. When the Klan's actions became too excessive even for the southern taste, members began leaving the Klan. Those who remained were usually individuals who had a pathological need to vent pain and injury on other humans. Outside pressure was placed upon the Klan, too. The activities of the white-sheeted vigilantes had made headlines across the country. An aroused public demanded that Washington take steps to stop the shameful acts. There were mass arrests, some confessions, and practically no convictions, but everyone knew the order was out to clamp down on the Klan.

In January 1869 the Klan's leader, Imperial Wizard Nathan Forest, dissolved the organization and ordered all the secret papers burned. Three years later the Klan had virtually disappeared. The fragments that still survived were vigilantes who felt a need to persecute, and they did so under the banner of a group no longer in existence. When President Rutherford B. Hayes ordered the withdrawal of the last divisions of the occupation army in 1877, the control of the South returned to the hands of the white southerners. New methods, less overt and more insidious, were used to prevent the blacks from taking their rightful place in society.

So it seemed the end had come to the Ku Klux Klan. The conditions that had encouraged its formation had changed and other means, less liable to prosecution, had been found to deal with the southerner's enemy: the blacks. The monster, however, was not dead but only hibernating until the climate was conducive to its awakening.

Eight years after the last official Klan robe had been packed away, William J. Simmons was born in Harpersville, Alabama. Simmons, as a child, was sickly and often had visions while in his sickbed.

"On horseback and in their white robes they rode across the wall in front of me," he later said. "As the picture faded I got down on my knees and swore that I would found a fraternal organization that would be a memorial to the Ku Klux Klan."

But that was in the future. During his young years, Simmons worked at a variety of jobs. He was in the Alabama Volunteers during the Spanish-American War. Later he served as an itinerant Methodist minister. Finally, he was a garter salesman. The field which was to prove most fertile for Simmons' talents, however, was that of professional organizer of fraternal groups. The Woodmen of the World, the Masons, the Spanish-American War Veterans, all were benefited by his talent. During this time the dream to form his own order lay at the back of Simmons' mind. Then an accident made him bedridden for three months, and he had the time to work out a detailed plan that he subsequently copyrighted. As a professional organizer, he knew the proper moment was needed to launch his idea.

The time came in the fall of 1915: the motion picture, *The Birth of a Nation,* directed by D. W. Griffith, was scheduled to open in a movie theater in Atlanta, Georgia. Atlanta had been burned by Union General Sherman during the Civil War. Even though the outrage had occurred more than fifty years before, the southerners had not forgotten. The motion picture showed how the vigilantism of the Ku Klux Klan had saved the South's honor by avenging a newly liberated black's attack on a white woman. Simmons was certain that the film would enflame memories that still smouldered in the minds of many of his compatriots and that men would come scurrying to enlist in his project.

The mood and timing seemed right, but the Renaissance of the Klan was not as auspicious as Simmons might have wished. Only fifteen men climbed the tremendous granite peak sixteen miles outside Atlanta on a cool November night to take part in the ceremony that Simmons had devised for the rebirth of the Klan. On the top of Stone Mountain, the men gathered rocks for a stone altar and for the base on which to mount the pine cross that Simmons had wrapped in excelsior and soaked with kerosene. At the proper moment in their ceremony the cross was ignited and its blazing form was visible for miles around. Similar crosses were soon to burn across the United States.

The flaming symbol represented the new Klan's emphasis on lifting certain sects of the Protestant church to an even higher level of importance. Direct attention to the repression of blacks was not a major goal, as that purpose was being well served by other means in the South. Support of thorough "Americanism" was stressed, however. During World War I sheeted Klansmen intervened in a Mobile, Alabama, shipyard strike. They also pursued draft dodgers, took part in patriotic parades, and chastised immoral women. Four years after its rebirth, the Klan's membership numbered several thousand. Simmons, knowing his earnings came solely from the membership dues, enlisted the help of Edward Young Clarke and Mrs. Elizabeth Tyler to swell the organization's ranks as well as his own wallet.

The team of Clarke and Tyler, known as the Southern

Publicity Association, divided the nation into sales districts. An army of recruiters was dispatched to ferret out new members. Their sales pitch was anti-Catholicism and, especially, pro-Americanism. Often a recruiter was advised to learn what was troubling a particular community and to offer the Klan as a sure remedy. The first person approached in an area was usually the Protestant minister. He was offered the post of Klan speaker. Hundreds yielded to the temptation. "Almost all of the national Klan lecturers were ministers," stated David M. Chalmers in *Hooded Americanism.*

The results of the Simmons, Clarke, and Tyler triumvirate were remarkable. By the summer of 1921 the Klan had added eighty-five thousand members. To profit even more from its activities, the Klan became what is known today as a conglomerate: a collection of diversified businesses under the same leadership. The Gate City Manufacturing Company in Atlanta, Georgia, was the official manufacturer of Klan costumes. The Klan used the Searchlight Publishing Company to print all its propaganda. A realty company was set up by Edward Young Clarke to control all the Klan's real estate holdings. Klan coffers were growing along with Klan popularity:

OKLAHOMA, 1922: Thirty thousand people cheered as a Klan airplane with a crimson cross on its wings flew over the Oklahoma City amusement park.

ARKANSAS, 1922: The Klan marched in a Texarkana parade, carrying placards which read "Law and

Order Must Prevail" and "We Stand For Old Glory and 100% Americanism."

TEXAS, 1922: The Klan has been credited with over five hundred tar-and-feather attacks and whippings as well as assorted threats, assaults and homicides.

The Klan, however, was not limited to the South and its bordering states. Members gathered from Portland, Maine, to Portland, Oregon, with Oregon boasting twenty-five thousand or more Klansmen. In Brooklyn, New York, the Klan found the safest place for its secret night meetings was the borough's traffic court chambers.

By the midtwenties the Klan could justly claim over three million members, a peak never before or since attained by any vigilante group. But signs of a decline were already evident. As usual with any form of mob justice, problems beset the Klan both from within and without.

Social conditions that had nourished the second wave of Klanism were changing. As the restlessness brought on by the First World War faded, Americans began to feel more settled. The peace that came after the war was an uneasy one, but it was peace.

Catholicism, the Klan's chief target, was proving not to be the threat people once thought. The hatred that had been aimed at the church was not necessarily caused by religious animosity. Many people feared that an alien power might come to control this country, and in this case papal rule was the dreaded outsider. Despite the Klan's speeches and literature that attempted to demonstrate how the pope was plotting an overthrow of the United States government, no actual evidence was available. Though the American people can at times be gullible and narrow-minded, they quickly tire of empty claims.

Lastly, a factor that is purely American, the heterogeneous society, worked against the organization. Waves of immigrants had arrived, but already they were being assimilated into the culture and were proving to be ambitious, productive individuals. The fright of being overrun by hordes of foreigners had been lessened by bills that Congress passed to limit the numbers of immigrants. People now felt that the government was aware of their concerns, and they did not need to turn to an illegal group for support.

The terrorist activities of the Klan repelled other members. Outsiders, too, were disgusted with the many accounts of people being burned alive, beaten, or scarred with acid. Even politicians who formerly had quietly ignored the Klan's tactics, appreciating the influence the vigilantes had with the voters, saw public attitudes were beginning to turn against the Klan.

Within the Klan itself there was growing disenchantment among the people who had joined it as a fraternal organization and were finding the Klan's activities less and less to their taste. There had been certain attractions to joining the secret fraternal group. For a ten dollar initiation fee, a member could attend meetings, wear a special costume, and use secret signs and codes. For those who lived a humdrum existence this excitement filled a void.

There was also somewhat of a sexual aura about the Klan's activities that seemed to appeal to puritanical white Protestants. Repressed individuals wrote and illustrated pamphlets that were actually hardcore pornography aimed at priests and nuns. Pictures could be drawn of sex activities and the perpetrators of the pictures would feel not guilt but, rather, elation, believing they were doing good. The Klan's physical attacks on people reeked of sadism as well as latent and overt homosexuality. Crowds gathered to watch the "wrongdoers" stripped of their clothing almost ceremoniously, and then beaten. In the cases of male blacks and Jews, often the sex organs were mutilated. Incidents of female rape by the Klansmen were frequent and sodomy was occasionally the final degradation inflicted upon males before murdering them. Eventually, many members were sickened by these excesses and left the Klan.

External events also blunted the thrill of belonging to an ultrasecret band. More and more, popular opinion was being mobilized against the Klan. Members preparing for a meeting with newly laundered sheets and secret words and codes would walk into the living room to say good-bye to their children. The youngsters, however, were gathered around the radio cheering for Bud Collyer as Superman defeating the hooded warriors. Worse, leaders engaged in open courtroom fights as they attempted to wrestle power into their own hands. States legislated anti-mask laws, forcing out members who were reluctant to march in parades without their faces covered. All these things happened over a period of fifteen or twenty years, during which the Klan fought for its life.

But attempts to infuse the flagging membership with new enthusiasm met with dismal failure. In 1925 a Klan parade of forty thousand members marched down Pennsylvania Avenue in Washington, D.C., but no upsurge in recruitment resulted from the nationwide publicity the parade received. The Klan hoped that the presidential election of 1928, in which Al Smith, a Roman Catholic, opposed Herbert Hoover, would be the impetus that would send people rushing back to Klan headquarters. The hope was fruitless. Smith was defeated not by the Klan and anti-Catholicism but by prosperity and Hoover's Republican party both of which were still strong throughout the country. Even the Klan's return to more social and fraternal activities in the early thirties did not lure back Klan dropouts.

From the late 1930s through the 1950s the pattern continued, and the weakened Klan finally splintered as a national organization. State vigilante leaders fought to make their particular Klan cell the dominant one which would resurrect the Klan. Beatings and lynchings, chiefly of blacks, continued through the 1930s and received considerable publicity, but by then the Klan had developed the reputation of being a strictly southern organization.

So the second surge of Klanism that had spread like an oil spill from the South to cover all the continental U.S. was defeated by the built-in weaknesses of the vigilante band. The KKK was slowly pushed back and contained to the lands below the Mason-Dixon line, and there it remains to this day.

But the Klan still breathes. Supreme Court decisions about school desegregation in the 1950s caused a slight rise in Klan popularity and activity as did the presence of civil rights workers in the South in the 1960s. Neither time, however, did the Klan gain sufficient strength to return it to its former power. Yet the danger exists that one day some social issue might arise that will create such strong fear among citizens that a third—and even deadlier—resurgence of the Klan could take place. In the Klan's own words:

> *Since Eighteen Hundred and Sixty-Six*
> *the KU KLUX KLAN*
> *has been riding and will*
> *continue to do so as long as*
> *the WHITE MAN liveth.*

5

The Threat of
Changing Moral Climate

Carry A. Nation

The United States has always been troubled by morality codes. The country is made up of a multitude of
cultures, religions, and nationalities, many having con-
flicting standards. Therefore what is considered right by
one group may be viewed as objectionable by others.
Citizens often have taken the law into their own hands
to force their own particular morality on a different
sector of the population. Such vigilante action tends to
be localized and not known to the rest of the country.
One vigilante, however, was so adamant that her campaign became famous worldwide.

The date was February 16, 1900; the place: Medicine
Lodge, Kansas. There were three women, but the tall
one, six feet and weighing a solid hundred and seventy-
five pounds, was obviously the leader. No one, least of
all frail Mr. O. L. Day had any doubts about that. The

three matrons had pushed their way into his pharmacy, shouting insults and threats. The leader had a voice that rose above the commotion when she called him "a fool and a rummy." Roughly, she shoved Day aside and entered the back room.

"Women," she yelled. "Here is the whiskey!"

Day tried to explain the ten-pound keg was not whiskey but "fine California Brandy."

"It's devil's brew to destroy the souls of men!" snapped the big woman.

Day silently thanked Heaven when the local marshal entered the room. In fact he felt so reassured by the presence of the law that he pushed the grim-faced female who now sat astride the keg. She one-armed him across the room without even getting to her feet. The marshal glanced at the crumpled druggist who lay in a corner, dazed. With practised skill, Marshal Gano threw a head-lock on the bespectacled woman.

"My neck's breaking!" she cried.

Before Gano could instruct her to cease resisting arrest, he heard a ripping noise. His torn coat fell from his back. Peering over his coatless shoulder, he saw the woman's two furious companions getting ready to do more serious damage to his person. Marshal Gano hastily retreated to the street.

The leader stood up. "Roll out the broth of hell."

The heavy keg grated across the floor, bouncing down into the street where a large group of onlookers had gathered. A heavy mallet was obtained from the local smithy. The Amazon-like female struck the keg "with such force," reported the Kansas *Journal*, "that liquor streamed out many feet into the air."

A cheer burst from the crowd. Some were pleased to see an end to at least a small amount of alcohol. Others whooped an expectant cheer as they stepped forward with cups to sample the loot. But the big leader grabbed a broom and swept the liquor into the gutter. As she set the brandy ablaze, more hurrahs and groans indicated once again the dual feelings of the people.

And so it would always be, for Carry Nation. Some cheered her hatchet-wielding battles against dispensaries of alcohol while others considered her quite demented.

If Carry Nation was not insane, she undeniably had a highly developed neurosis. She was violently against alcohol, tobacco, sex, and the Masonic Lodge, and she harbored many lesser hates as well. To question Carry's mental state is valid even though her biographers, as she did herself, either deny any irregularities or avoid the question altogether. Certainly, the woman had suffered enough by the time she had matured to cause a complete and irreversible psychological disorder.

Carry Amelia Moore was born on November 25, 1846, in Garrard County, Kentucky. She was later to have five smaller brothers and sisters. Her mother's manner had always been aloof and formal, but, following Carry's birth, Mrs. Moore announced to her astounded family that she was a lady-in-waiting to Queen Victoria. Events moved quickly in Mrs. Moore's disturbed mind; before long she believed she *was* Queen Victoria, and began to dress and act the part. Regal gowns of purple velvet replaced her aprons and housedresses, and one day she rode forth in the Moores' horse and buggy, to pay a royal visit, she announced, to the King of Belgium.

George Moore, Carry's father, was a kind though ineffectual man who forever wanted to be somewhere else. During Carry's formative years the family zig-zagged and backtracked across the West and Midwest. From Dix River, Kentucky, where Carry had been born, the Moores moved to Danville and then to Midway and on again to Cass County, Missouri. On the trip from Kentucky to Missouri, Carry developed a cold that grew progressively worse. A year in a sick bed while living in Missouri did not improve her condition.

One day the girl, more dead than alive, was placed aboard a wagon and taken to a revival meeting. After hours of fervent hymn singing and exhortations, the evangelistic leader begged converts to step forward. Suffering terrible pain, Carry stumbled and dragged herself down the aisle, to be received by the open-armed revivalist. Two days later, she was taken from her sick bed and brought to an ice-fringed stream. While everyone thanked God for guiding the child to their flock, Carry was dunked into frigid water over her head.

Two results were produced by the encounter with this firebrand variety of religion. Twelve-year-old Carry became determined to live a pure and sanctimonious life. Also she was bedridden for the next five years. During this period Carry had visions. She saw snakes and angels, and held lengthy discussions with the latter. While still abed, she felt an overpowering urge to spread the gospel. She rounded up a captive audience of black slaves on Sunday afternoons and lectured them about sin and God.

As if Carry did not already have enough to bear, her father decided the moment was ripe for another move. For six weeks the family wagon bumped along hot, dusty roads to Grayson County, Texas, where Mr. Moore bought a farm. Bad luck continued to plague the family, for almost immediately all the horses and mules died from an unknown disease. In George Moore's estimation there was only one thing to do. Sell the farm and move back to Missouri. Once more they made the unpleasant trek. One side benefit of the arduous traveling was that Carry inexplicably underwent a swift and complete recovery. By the time the family reached Missouri, she glowed with good health. The return of her strength was fortunate because the Moores found Missouri in the grip of the Civil War. Moore freed his slaves and took his loved ones into an Army post in Kansas City.

With the younger Moore children attending school and Mrs. Moore, still believing she was Queen Victoria, too vague to do any house chores, Carry had to handle the cooking and cleaning. In her spare time she worked as a volunteer nurse at a hospital for wounded soldiers.

During this period, while Carry was in her late teens, a school teacher came to live with the Moore family. Dr. Charles Gloyd had been trained as a physician, but he found more frequent employment as an educator. In one of Mrs. Moore's rare moments of lucidity before she was committed to the Missouri State Hospital for the Insane, she forbade her daughter and Charles Gloyd ever to be alone together in the same room. The Moore house was small, and as Carry and Gloyd tried to obey the mother's proclamation, humorous situations developed with one person entering a room from one door as another fled through a different exit. Eventually, both Carry and Charles tired of this farcical behavior, and on November 21, 1867, four days before her twenty-first birthday, Carry Amelia Moore became Carry Gloyd. Prophetically, Gloyd was drunk on his wedding day.

"I had no idea of the curse of rum," Carry subsequently wrote. "I did not fear anything, for I was in love, and doubted him in nothing."

Drinking soon became the major activity of Gloyd's days and nights. When he found no drinking partners around home, he took to the village streets. Within a year, pregnant Carry, dingy shawl pulled around her shoulders, was a familiar nighttime sight as she scoured the town for her alcohol-loving husband. The doors of the Masonic headquarters were subjected to violent poundings as Carry raucously demanded that Gloyd be returned.

As if a drunken spouse was not enough of a tribulation, Carry's daughter, Charlien, was afflicted with disabilities that had little precedent in medical history. In early childhood, the girl's right jaw became badly swollen. A festering sore was found to be eating its way through the cheek. All sorts of medical and home remedies were tried to no avail. Charlien's right cheek fell out, leaving her teeth bare. For nine long days Charlien teetered on the brink of death.

Doctors and a minister advised Carry it would be better if the child died, for if she survived she would be horribly deformed. Carry would have none of their con-

solations. She believed her prayers would be answered.
The force of Carry's determination may have been ab-
sorbed by the patient because the sore slowly healed
until the hole was about the size of a quarter. Charlien's
agony had only begun, however. Though the sore was
healing, her jaws clamped shut and would not open
again for eight years.

Her father never knew of Charlien's problems, for he
died in the 1870s. Carry suffered a period of financial
setbacks. She did manage to scrape together enough
money to attend a normal school. Following graduation
she was hired for a teaching position from which she
was fired when she quarreled with a school-board member about the correct sound for the letter "a." The last
situation was ironic, for words beginning with "A" were
to weave in and out of Carry's career. Her own middle
name began with the letter. Alcohol had ruined her
first marriage and would soon be the key word of her
professional scraps. And, David A. Nation was about
to walk onstage.

David Nation was a Civil War veteran who, at the
time he met Carry, was acting-editor of a small-town
paper. Nation, almost twenty years older than Carry,
was a widower with a family of his own. Though Carry's
friends opposed the marriage, Carry thought she knew
best and married David in 1877. About the only thing
Carry was to gain from the marriage was a name useful
to her when she became an active reformer. "Carry
A. Nation" was what her name and conscience bid her
to do. The phrase became a campaign slogan, her name
a legend.

Her friends were proven right. If Carry had been bad off before meeting Nation, she was worse after she had married him. The couple moved to Texas where they bought seventeen hundred acres near the San Bernardo River. David quarreled with a neighbor who retaliated by tossing all the Nations' plows and farming tools into the river. In the spring all of David's horses died and a hired hand absconded with the little cash the family had. With all these problems arising, Nation decided he would return to his original profession of attorney-at-law. He moved to Columbia, Texas, and soon after Carry and Charlien and Lola Nation, a stepdaughter, joined him there, and Carry became tenant-operator of a broken-down hotel.

Under Carry's management, the Columbia Hotel snared a few guests. At least it was a source of income, which the Nations badly needed since David had found few clients. Carry worked, literally, from dawn to midnight: washing, cooking, cleaning, and killing rats. Spells of depression and hysterical fits began to seize her. Her memory failed so badly that at times she could not remember her own name. Insomnia alternated with fearful nightmares of snakes that coiled about her, striking repeatedly, dreadful dreams from which she would awaken screaming.

To escape the nightmares, Carry passed her nights at the window, staring at the saloon across the road. Over and over, she wondered how different her life would now be if alcohol had not claimed Gloyd.

A slightly more lucrative job opened in Richmond, Texas, where Carry would manage a twenty-one-room hotel and six cottages. The Nations journeyed to Fort Bend County. Not only were the usual members of the family dependent upon Carry, but her aging father moved in as did Charlien's husband. The responsibility and work load was staggering for Carry. Delusions completely engulfed her. She would wander the streets of Richmond, asking any passerby, "Do you love God?"

Two bizarre incidents were to firmly establish in Carry's mind the belief that she was a recipient of Heavenly guidance. A drought had caused great hardship to Fort Bend County for years. Carry decided to end the natural disaster. She announced at the Methodist church that a prayer meeting would be held to "offer supplications for additional moisture." At the session, Carry begged, threatened, and cajoled the Powers to deliver rain. In full confidence, she adjourned the convocation and went outdoors to check on her success.

"After the meeting we were standing on the platform in front of the church," she was to write in her autobiography, "when a sprinkle of rain fell on the platform and on the shutters of the house." The soft gentle rain continued for the next three days.

If water was involved in the first strange episode, it was fire the next time.

In March 1889, Carry was summoned by a roomer in the middle of the night. The elderly man complained of violent stomach pains. Carry prepared a mustard plaster which she applied to the man's aching belly. As she started for her own room, she saw "a light behind me, which would come and go in flashes." There was no natural cause for the flickering so Carry marked it up to a vision. The following day she solemnly warned each member of her family that trouble was coming.

The next night at the exact same time she had seen the light the previous night, the town of Richmond awoke to find half the village on fire. Flames leaped from building to building, devouring whole blocks of the wooden structures. The guests in Carry's hotel grabbed what few belongings they could and fled for safety. As one old woman rushed through the lobby, she spied Carry sitting in a rocker as if relaxing after a hard day's work.

"That woman has lost her mind!" the old lady moaned as she rushed outdoors into the smoke-filled street.

Guests and family members begged Carry to come with them. The building's destruction was imminent. Carry refused, saying quietly that no harm would come to her. There was no time left to argue with the obstinate woman. Everyone ran outside where the crackle and roar from the fire was tremendous. Yet many citizens later testified that above the noise they heard Carry's booming voice singing hymns.

The red and yellow flames were now two houses away. Next, the building adjacent to the hotel went. And then . . . the fire stopped advancing. The blaze weakened and soon darkened into smouldering embers. Carry and her hotel had been spared.

As incidents like this began to spread her fame through the Midwest, Carry managed a business deal in which she swapped her hotel in Texas for property in Medicine Lodge, Kansas. Better business and more visions came Carry's way. Her application for sainthood was rejected by all recognized sects, but her intense religious fervor grew even stronger. There were periods when Carry completely lost touch with reality. Other times she would lock herself in the basement for days on end. Her family would hear her prayers, boisterous singing, and strange shrieks.

Abruptly, the wildness ended. Carry emerged from this latest and most-possessed spell with a quiet, but intense hatred of alcohol, tobacco, and illicit sex. But, now, in addition to believing these evils had to be eliminated, she felt certain that *she* had been the one selected to do the job. Fifty-four-year-old Carry A. Nation was about to march—hatchet in hand—into the pages of history.

At this point Carry Nation fit the qualifications of the typical vigilante. Her full-blown monomania convinced her that she was in the right and that which she opposed was completely wrong. Authorities were doing nothing to alleviate the problem. Kansas was a dry state. Since the 1880s the sale of alcohol was against state law unless it was for "medicinal, scientific and mechanical purposes." People managed to get around this law. Druggists were constantly dispensing whiskey as a remedy for the bubonic plague or for leprosy or, most ironically of all, as a "refillable prescription for chronic alcoholism." Saloons and "joints" openly flourished. As long as a monthly fine was faithfully paid, the authorities made no effort to close down the establishments.

With all this knowledge in hand, Carry began her campaign. The testing ground was Medicine Lodge, the highpoint being the attack on O. L. Day's pharmacy. Having an innate dramatic sense, Carry knew that these minor-league skirmishes were a healthy beginning, but that she would have to attract more attention in order to broaden her base of support. She was the county president of the Woman's Christian Temperance Union, but they were pacifists as far as she was concerned. The headquarters in Evanston, Illinois, did not condone the kind of militant actions Carry undertook. After her initial success at Medicine Lodge, Carry struck again in another small Kansas town, Kiowa. Then she aimed her sights higher. Wichita.

Wichita, Kansas, had survived Marshal Wyatt Earp's gun duels as well as assorted bandits like Rowdy Joe Lowe and Shanghai Pierce, but the residents would long remember the chilling invasion of the hymn-singing reformer, Carry A. Nation.

In less than an hour Carry had reduced the Annex of the Hotel Carey to ruins. The room was knee-deep in broken glass and reeked of whiskey and beer. A fifteen hundred dollar Victorian mirror was smashed. A nude painting of Cleopatra was gashed by a ragged tear the size of a three-inch rock. Deep dents had been hacked into the cherrywood bar and the crystal chandelier had cast its last warm, inviting glow.

Carry was promptly marched off to jail, singing, "Stand up, stand up for Jesus / Ye soldiers of the cross." While officials debated their next step, she befriended the prisoners in nearby cells. The drunks, thieves, and murderers were so taken with her hymn singing and prayer sessions that they collaborated on a nine-stanza poem. One stanza read:

> Some who'd never know a mother,
> Ne'er had learned to kneel and pray,
> Raised their hands, their face to cover,
> Till her words had died away.

While Carry was rounding up imprisoned disciples, Wichita law officials saw no exit from their quandary. Carry had wrecked the hotel bar. The business, however, was an illegal one under Kansan law. How could they prosecute Carry without doing the same to the bar proprietor? And if they did that—and antagonized all the bar owners—they would lose all the monthly fine money as well as places to drink. To make matters more complicated, Carry had popular support, both locally and countrywide. Such an honored editor as William Allen White of the Emporia (Kansas) *Gazette* wrote: "Fight the devil with fire. Smash the joints with hatchets. Drive the jointists from Kansas. They have no rights that a white man is bound to respect. Hurray for Carry Nation!" In addition the Evanston, W.C.T.U. headquarters, despite their stand against militancy, had sent very vocal representatives to stand by their newsmaking member. Worse, many people in Wichita had at last found a leader to head their cause.

At length the charges were dropped, and Carry was released on January 12, 1901. Nine days later she reappeared in Wichita mainly to address the local W.C.T.U.

chapter. Her speech was so inspiring that a detachment of females with Carry in the lead smashed two saloons. Their rampage came to an abrupt end, however, when the owner of the second bar leveled a revolver at Carry's temple. She decided retreat would be the wisest move at that point.

Undaunted, Carry regrouped her forces and headed for her first target: the bar in the Hotel Carey. Once again she was arrested. The following afternoon, after paying the $1,000 bail, Carry set out for the railroad depot. Few people have had such a boisterous sendoff. The crowd was mixed in its feelings, however. Some threw compliments; others threw eggs. Head high, already planning her next assault, Carry stepped aboard the train.

On January 23, 1901, Carry visited Enterprise, Kansas. She was pelted with rotten eggs and received a black eye from the wife or mistress of a saloon owner. But her next stop was Topeka, the state capital. Carry brought her campaign to the state legislature by destroying the bar in the Senate building.

Thanks to Carry Nation, within a month's time not only the city of Topeka but the entire state of Kansas was on the brink of rebellion. Prohibitionists and anti-prohibitionists formed gangs, arming themselves with clubs, hatchets, guns, and battering rams. Countergroups met on street corners and brawls broke out. The governor considered bringing the militia into the capital and putting the entire state under martial law.

With so many underlings heeding the call of battle, Carry now embarked on a lecture tour to bring her message to the whole country. Missouri, Iowa, Ohio were included in the whistle-stop tour. The pattern was much the same wherever she went: A fire and brimstone speech, followed, usually, by a token attack on a saloon with Carry leading the group in a hymn and being allowed to take the first swing with her hatchet.

To pay expenses Carry had contracted with a Rhode Island manufacturer for toy hatchets made out of pewter, which she sold for ten cents or a quarter, depending upon the economic level of her audience. The bigger cities felt the force of Carry's words and ax-swinging arm. Chicago and New York City were told about the glory of "hatchetation," a term Carry coined and the title of an unproduced play she wrote. Europe beckoned. Carry answered. And then back across the Atlantic she sailed to revisit New York City and Washington.

While Carry invaded large cities, the grassroots movement continued the work-a-day battles. In Boston, Mrs. Mary Green rushed into a saloon, shouting, "I'm Carry Nation and I'll leave no rum shops in this town!" Whereupon she threw a plateful of free lunch into the bartender's face and a billiard ball through the mirror. A black named Benjamin Levy in Oyster Bay, New York, ransacked a bar, claiming he had been inspired by Carry Nation. Five enraged members of the W.C.T.U. invaded two bars in Dalton, Arkansas, and left scenes of wreckage behind them.

On January 13, 1911, Carry, now sixty-four, mounted a platform in Eureka Springs, Missouri. Her voice was strong; her message stronger. Carry paused, her forehead knotted as if confused. She lifted a hand to a cheek.

The audience gasped for fear she might faint. Several people on the platform offered to assist her down, but she politely refused all help—the spirit that had kept her in a hotel rocker as a fire bore down still lived in her.

In a slow, barely audible voice, she said, "I have done what I could."

Then Carry Nation collapsed into the arms of a friend. Five months later she was dead.

If prohibition was her goal, there were and still are monuments to Carry Amelia Nation. Though she did not live to see it, a Constitutional Amendment against alcohol was passed in 1918 and the entire United States went dry. This would never have come about without Carry's hatchet-swinging attacks, for no one had alerted the country to the temperance cause as Carry had. And, thanks to Carry Nation, the state of Kansas is dry to this day. These are the sort of memorials Carry would have enjoyed. There have been others.

Carry was buried in an unmarked grave beside her mother. Twelve years after her death, a group of friends collected money for a granite marker to be erected over the Belton, Missouri, grave. The inscription paraphrased Carry's last public utterance: "She Hath Done What She Could." There was another testimonial. A handsome, inscribed fountain was built on the spot where she had first been arrested in Wichita. But a runaway, oversized beer truck later smashed the monument.

Even worse, one can almost hear a loud, yet ghostly voice denouncing this June 11, 1972, *New York Times* item:

HOMETOWN OF W.C.T.U.
GETS LIQUOR LICENSES

EVANSTON, Ill., June 10—The barkeep's traditional cry that it's time for one for the road was heard early this morning for the first time in 117 years in this Chicago suburb—the home of the Woman's Christian Temperance Union.

The W.C.T.U. has promised to go to court to keep its hometown dry.

As the newspaper article indicates, vigilantes seeking to impose their morality code on everyone are still present in the United States. This type of vigilante group tries to prevent the distribution or showing of movies, stage presentations, or literature that offends its own often rigid standards. Or it destroys a park in Queens, New York, in an attempt to drive away homosexuals.

Through the efforts of vigilantes like these, numerous state and local laws and ordinances have been enacted over the years. Disliked by a growing number of law-enforcement officers, such laws result in what are known as "victimless crimes"—crimes in which the only offense to society is the personal moral code of the individual or individuals involved.

VIGILANTISM IN AMERICA TODAY

6

Contemporary Vigilantism

There is something old-fashioned sounding about the word "vigilantism." The term usually brings to mind a band of cowboys dragging a suspected cattle rustler or horse thief from the town jail and "stringing him up." But vigilantism is still with us, its restless, dissatisfied, vengeful character ever at the ready.

Restlessness does not belong to vigilantes alone; it has always been a typical characteristic of Americans. For restlessness is an element of the pioneering spirit that from the very beginning of this country's history responded to the compelling challenge of a vast land. Pioneers brought vitality and progress to the new country. They traveled to new territories and settled there. Their children and grandchildren grew up in the new area. Cities rose and prospered.

Present-day Americans are still vastly motivated by

restlessness. "At least a fifth of all Americans move one or more times each year; and the pace of the movement of Americans is still increasing," writes Vance Packard in *A Nation of Strangers*. But an aura of sadness and futility often seems to surround present-day mobility.

Individuals and families move from one place to another in search of a happy fulfillment of their needs or wants or dreams, but usually they find no substantial change, no sense of a new start. And even as a man or woman slips from job to job, locality to locality, there is a feeling that the new move, too, is temporary. The next home is not envisioned as a permanent residence for future generations. Instead it is inspected for its resale value as a business investment. Also, the environments available to Americans have narrowed and are now more sharply defined as rural, suburban, or urban —and these, by their very natures, have sometimes produced problems that lead to vigilantism.

Another quality of life in the United States in the 1970s that can give rise to vigilantism is the extremist approach to social problems that has beset the country. The November 1963 assassination of President John F. Kennedy threw the country into an emotional tailspin that still has not been fully corrected. There followed more assassinations, riots, a devastating war, political scandal. And with each succeeding outbreak of madness, the people appeared to be affected less and less. While Americans seem to have become daily more hardened to each other's human needs, they have become more and more determined that what *they* want, individually or collectively, must be made to come about immediately. Persons who once would have lived out their days in an atmosphere of relative quiet, complaining only in the privacy of their homes, now take to the streets with placards and sometimes with bombs. This new, more impatient frame of mind has frequently aided the cause of vigilantism.

The remaining chapters of this exploration of vigilantism in America will center, then, on the environments in which people in the U.S. today reside—Rural, Suburban, and Urban—and on the major areas of social concern that are currently creating problems for the people of the United States.

Although the environments and the nature of the country's troubles may be different from those that gave rise to the vigilantism of America's past, similarities exist between the old and the new vigilantism—not only in the causes but in the purposes, as well. The San Francisco Committee that employed vigilantism to topple a political party has its counterparts in many modern cities. Racist vigilantes still use turbulent conditions as an excuse for venting their hatred upon other groups. Carry Nation's exuberance is matched by today's defenders of morality who still seek to impose their particular code of behavior on everyone. And, unfortunately, America today is no better off for having vigilantes who take the law into their own hands than it was in the past.

7

Today:
Rural Vigilantes

The social milieu today that most closely resembles nine-teenth-century America is the rural farm area. The economy is still predominantly agricultural though many men work days at nearby urban-situated factories or are self-employed in service fields like plumbing or carpentry. The officials of the small town, such as law enforcement, bank, and school personnel, are more highly respected than in suburban or urban areas, but at the same time are expected to follow a stricter code of conduct. Usually they reside in the town proper, often being obligated to do so if they wish to hold the job. Governmental inroads are feared unless a natural disaster affects the crops or homes, and then outside aid is expected to be immediately forthcoming.

Day-to-day living has not changed drastically since the 1800s. Social life revolves around a nucleus of church-related activities, such as choir practice or turkey suppers or cake sales. Visits to friends or relatives in summer and lengthy television viewing in winter comprise the remainder of the rural family's leisure time.

If the rural inhabitants are not urbanites who have fled the "rat race," they tend to be very similar to their forebears of a century ago. Independent and self-reliant, they are highly suspicious of outsiders and hostile to those who do not work. On the surface they seem extremely moral, their standards following the dictates of a particular Protestant or Roman Catholic church. The town is still populated with "good" and "bad" families. Offspring of good families will, in everyone's estimation, find a useful slot when they mature. Sons and daughters of bad families, though they are pitied for having such poor parents, are generally seen as headed for a life of loafing or crime or sexual looseness.

Paramount in the rural individual's mind is the feeling that anything that disrupts this life-style or negates his or her values is the enemy. An enemy can be dealt with in several ways. Defense may come as social ostracism or economic hindrances. Storekeepers might refuse to permit credit or claim not to have a desired item in stock. If the situation is extreme, then the people band together to take more direct action. All these tactics constitute vigilantism in some form. With transient America rapidly changing in mores and economic drives, rural areas are feeling increasing pressure to change. They react accordingly.

Consider this incident that took place in a rural area of upper New York State. A man who shall be called

Hank lived on the same one hundred and fifty acres his family had farmed since the late 1880s. Over the years he had sold bits of it, holding the mortgages in his name. Farming is cyclical with good years and, unfortunately, bad ones. If a family could not meet a month's payment, Hank shrugged and told them to try the next month. The people who were in debt to Hank for the most part appreciated his thoughtfulness. If they missed a few months' payments, they made sure that any money that came in was immediately set aside to pay some of their debt.

The rural area was in balance. But one cold January night Hank died of a heart attack. All his estate went to his sixty-four-year-old sister who had left the farm when she was in her early teens. The woman, who shall be called Elizabeth, had attended normal school and worked all her life as a mathematics teacher. Now retired, Lizzie returned to the old homestead. Her plan was to live out her life there once she had straightened out her deceased brother's money matters. She saw many mortgages far in arrears and concluded Hank had been duped by ne'er-do-wells. She began insisting upon prompt monthly payments.

Lizzie was not a villain. Her analytical mind was trained to deal with a different system of checks and balances. In the urban area where she lived money borrowed was paid back on time. As she saw it, all monetary minuses had to be balanced at scheduled periods with pluses.

The people in the area viewed Elizabeth as a heartless, money-mad woman. After all, she was getting social security checks and a teacher's pension so she was not strapped for money as were some of the farmers. Worse, Elizabeth had forsaken the area when young to live in a city. She was no longer one of them.

The first mode of vigilantism Lizzie encountered was social ostracism when the women informally agreed to "have nothing to do with her." True, if they met her face to face in the market, they spared Elizabeth a forced smile and a cool hello. But no friendly calls were made or invitations extended.

After a few months Lizzie felt the effect of these tactics. She had changed her mind about permanently living on the farm. Once the title to the property was clear, she would put her real estate holdings on the market. But first the mortgages had to be organized.

Her lawyers dispatched notices informing the debtors that if within a specified amount of time the mortgage payments were not brought up to date, Elizabeth would be forced to foreclose. Some farmers desperately hunted for additional funds, but with no success. Elizabeth was unmoved by their explanations about the delayed payments. More than ever she wanted to escape the homestead. Also, she suspected that what she was hearing were the same sob stories her brother had given into over the years. She informed her lawyer to start court proceedings. Six mortgages were foreclosed and the people were evicted.

Local people became increasingly angry. Months later Lizzie sold the buildings and land as farm property. Only another six to eight weeks and she would go to "closing" and be away from that place forever.

Late one February night when the temperature had dropped to below zero and five feet of snow lay on the ground, Lizzie was awakened by a bright light flickering on her bedroom wall. She rushed to the window. The barn was on fire. Even though the fire department was there within minutes, the structure was too far gone to be saved. The sale became void because the property had been sold as a farm, but without the barn it would be impossible to have a working farm.

Within a year Lizzie resold the property at a good price and moved to a city apartment where she is happy. Almost all the country dwellers still reside on their farms, their lives continuing along the same, comfortable lines of many years. But there remains the question of the fire.

"Must've been some kids playing with matches," suggested a fireman.

At two o'clock in the morning? In the dead of winter? That explanation does not seem too substantial. The local farmers only smile when asked about the fire. One crusty oldtimer offered, "Some people can get real mad when forced off their land."

The struggle between Elizabeth and her rural neighbors was unfortunate because both she and the farmers were basically decent people. No one was motivated by greed or selfishness at the beginning. But neither side was able to understand the other. Two life-styles had met and clashed. The rise of vigilantism had only intensified the problems.

Opposite life-styles led to another eruption of rural vigilantism, but this time in a form not usually recognized as vigilantism. Recent newcomers to the sparsely settled areas of this country have been the communes that began in California and the Southwest around 1964. By 1969 the movement had reached the cooler areas of the U.S., such as the Middle Atlantic and New England states.

Communes are most often formed by young people, usually in their late teens or twenties, who buy or rent a house and live together as a loosely knit "family." Often the commune is composed of a mixed group who for individual reasons seek the comfort of a family of peers. The reasons are as varied as the people who join. A common desire among some young people to return to the simpler, pastoral life might be the unifying reason for forming a commune. The members then turn their backs on middle-class values and the gospel of success that they feel have brought so much emotional unhappiness to the older generation. Sometimes the group has religious philosophies different from the established sects and wishes to find a location where members can worship as they wish.

Psychologists explain that communes can fill a definite need. Too often a commune group is the first family the individual finds where he is accepted for himself and is free from constant negative criticism. These youngsters frequently have been driven from their own homes by conflicts arising between generations.

The youth commune usually seeks out a place away from the centers of civilization, as twenty men and fourteen women did in 1969. They bought an old three-story farmhouse on a dirt road about eight miles from Meadville, Pennsylvania, the county seat of Crawford county up in the northwest corner of the state. Thus, Oz, a commune designed for religious freedom was born. The name came from a story by L. Frank Baum who used Oz as the name for his magical land "somewhere over the rainbow."

From the outset the group was aware that they might have trouble with the local inhabitants. Other communes had certainly run into problems along that line. The leaders decided that the commune should be open to visitors so that everyone could see that Oz was merely a band of ordinary people trying to lead their lives according to their own principles. This approach seemed to work well. Each weekend lines of cars would approach the commune. The outsiders would be welcomed and given an unofficial tour. The site soon proved so attractive that state police were called in to control the illegal parking and the traffic jams.

The food of the commune came from the land. A few local farmers who learned that the Ozians were not troublemakers gave advice and help with the agricultural efforts.

"They were great workers and good people," said one local man who had taught the young people some basic facts about farming.

And the young inhabitants of Oz appreciated the outside assistance and admired the older men. "The farmers have the same respect for nature as we do," a young man told a reporter.

But small signs of trouble began to appear. Some local residents became upset when their own children ran away to join the commune. The leader of Oz said he must have counseled hundreds of unhappy youngsters who felt commune life was for them. Most children returned home a bit more contented. The parents, however, rather than undergoing self-examination, blamed the commune for their children's dissatisfaction.

The day came when the commune members decided to visit Meadville to see what the city of some twenty thousand inhabitants was like. Meadville is similar to most urban areas surrounded by distinctly rural territory. It has a First Baptist Church, a few bars, and many green-and-white litter cans. Politically, the city is a Republican stronghold. The sight of the barefooted communers stepping down from their painted school bus stopped traffic and business in the city. As the bearded young men and the girls in their long, flapping dresses passed along the sidewalks, shoppers stood and gaped.

When the local residents returned to their farms, they began talking about the commune's members. Americans tend to distrust anyone who speaks, acts, or dresses uniquely. The rural families around Oz were true to the pattern. First, they mentioned the group's oddness, but as the tales moved from parlor to pasture, fear began to color the content. Untrue stories spread over the countryside like a swarm of locusts.

"All drug addicts," one farmer told his friend.

"There've been a lot of thefts around here since the group moved in," inferred another.

One woman insisted that she had seen "a pack of them drag a sixteen-year-old into the weeds."

More violent anticommune feelings were expressed. Whether these incidents were part of an organized drive against Oz or simply unconnected episodes is difficult to tell. If they were not planned, the thread of emotion that wove them together reflected the mood of the residents of the area.

The first hint of this underlying feeling occurred when three drunken motorcyclists rode along the dirt road and shot a rifle at the commune. When an elderly farmer who had befriended the Ozians tried to dispel the cyclists, they beat him. The next indication of hostility came one morning while everyone in the commune was asleep. One or more people sneaked into the old house and set a mattress on fire. Luckily, the smoke awoke some members, and the fire was doused before the wooden structure was seriously damaged. Soon after a pet dog was found shot. Then a gang of youths tried to drag a girl who was a commune member into their car. When she refused and struggled free, they sliced her face with a razor.

As these events followed one after another, the "Great Hepatitis Scare" took hold. One commune member was found to have infectious hepatitis. Area residents were certain that the whole commune would fall ill and probably had already started an epidemic that would sweep the county.

A protest meeting was called at the Summit Township Fire Hall. The announcement read: "All Citizens Welcome." But the democratic process in that Pennsylvania community apparently did not include persons from a *commune,* for when a group arrived from Oz only two members were allowed to enter. So the discussion about whether or not the commune ought to be allowed to remain in the county was decidedly one-sided at that gathering of citizens in the Summit Township Fire Hall. But nothing definite was voted on during the meeting.

Unfortunately, months would pass before the health department would release the figures showing that the year of Oz's presence brought only nine cases of hepatitis compared to the non-Ozian year before when there had been fifteen. Clearly Oz did not cause an upswing in the incidence of the illness in the locality.

The form of vigilantism that ultimately destroyed Oz is perhaps the most insidious and the most difficult form to control because it is legally proper. It is also frighteningly immoral. The means is to employ a law-enforcement body to rout the enemy by some quirk of legality. In the case of Oz, an 1869 statute was unearthed and used as the basis for an invasion of the premises by state troopers, who arrested the members of the commune for "maintaining a disorderly house."

The one hundred-year-old law labeled any building a "disorderly house" wherein idleness, gaming, drinking, common nuisances, or disturbing the neighborhood was found to be encouraged. If this law were to be enforced countrywide, whole towns could conceivably be cleared of their inhabitants. But around Meadville, Pennsylvania, the accusing finger pointed only at Oz. It was the one and only habitation in the entire area that any local citizen felt he or she could readily identify as a "disorderly house." So the state police duly arrested all the adults of the commune and turned the children of Oz over to the juvenile authorities to be cared for.

The court agreed to drop the charges if the members of Oz left the area, a solution reminiscent of the San Francisco Vigilance Committees' sentencing of their prisoners to jail, but then offering them exile as a means of escape. The Ozians accepted the court's offer.

Its search for happiness having failed, the Oz family broke up. Some youngsters returned home, hoping conditions would be more tolerable than before. Of these, most were soon to be on the road again. Others drifted across the country, seeking another commune. There were also those who, lost without the stabilizing influence of the Oz family, sought the deceptive consolation of drugs.

Oz has not been the only victim of so-called authorized vigilantism. Another group has for more than a hundred years felt the vigilantes' blows: the southern blacks.

Immediately after the Civil War, as an earlier chapter related, the blacks were frightened away from the ballot box by the Ku Klux Klan and its spin-off gangs. When the reins of power were handed back to the true southerner following the withdrawal of Union occupation forces, less obvious means were employed to prevent the blacks from voting. All these tactics, open or secretive, can be viewed as a form of vigilantism. Certain people, in this case the southern whites, felt something had to be done to control their enemy: the blacks. The whites feared the power the blacks could exercise if they were allowed to vote. Recognized authorities—the federal government—were doing nothing to prevent potential black rule of the South, so the white folks felt they had to handle the danger themselves. Though no official vigilante band was formed, members of the white population were united by the feelings they shared.

Having forced the slaves to remain uneducated before the Civil War, the postwar South knew that most black adults still could not read or write. So the states passed laws designed to prevent blacks from voting. Any person who wanted to vote in any election had to be able to pass a literacy test. These qualifying exams automatically eliminated many black voters. The southern conspiracy also had foresight. In the not-too-far future the children of the former slaves would be reaching an age when they could vote. These potential ballot-casters *would* be able to write and read and therefore pass the literacy test. So educational systems of separate schools for whites and blacks were organized with two goals in mind. First, the prejudiced whites would not have their children associated with blacks. Second, the white schools would have the better-trained teachers and ample supplies while the facilities for blacks would be ineffective, producing poorly equipped graduates.

If, however, some blacks managed to become educated despite the efforts of the southern schools, another official block was thrown in their path: the poll tax. Anyone who wished to vote had to pay a nominal fee. In Virginia, the tax was $1.50 with the other southern states

setting similar amounts. For a family living on a middle-
or better-than-average income, the poll tax was negli-
gible. But for those individuals who barely had enough
money to provide food and shelter, a dollar and fifty
cents can be a financial drain. Besides, even if a black
had the money to pay the poll tax, of what practical
value would it be to pay money to vote for a slate of
candidates, none of whom would have the blacks' interests in mind?

Reports of these unfair strategies occasionally found
their way into the news media, but most people remained unconcerned about the blacks' plight. With no
ground swell of emotion from their constituencies, most
federal politicians felt no need to take steps to help
the blacks. In 1939, however, a constitutional amendment was proposed that would abolish poll taxes as a
prerequisite for voting in federal elections. The slow
process for adopting a new amendment was initiated,
but the war years came and more pressing problems
faced the nation.

Both blacks and whites returned from the battlefields
of World War II and Korea with new spirit and goals.
A persecuted people began to find leadership and allies.
During the late nineteen-forties and into the fifties,
strides were taken to free the blacks. The country as a
whole became more aware of the undemocratic situation
in the South. Finally, in 1962, twenty-three years after
the Twenty-fourth Amendment was first offered, the
law became part of the Constitution. No poll taxes were
permitted in a federal election. But the ruling did not
affect local or state elections.

Three years later the Voting Rights Act of 1965 abolished the poll tax and literacy tests. Southern blacks were aided by the northern civil rights workers who traveled south to help with voter registration. Blacks, slowly at first, then in greater numbers began to vote, and black candidates bravely announced their intention to run for office.

Vigilantism did not accept these setbacks calmly. The fight was not without its defeats and victims. Hardboiled southern politicians would coldly ignore blacks seeking to vote unless federal marshals intervened. Midnight terrorists would try to intimidate blacks by flinging anything from bags of garbage to Molotov cocktails at them. Welfare officials would deny government-supplied food to needy blacks. In June 1964 three young civil rights workers were kidnapped by a vigilante mob, murdered, and buried on a dam construction site in Mississippi. The mob was later found to have included the local sheriff and other law-enforcement officials.

As recently as 1971 blacks and whites who volunteered to help bring out eligible black voters were still being harassed. Edgar Higginbottom, age twenty-five, Eldit McClinton, age thirty-two, and Jo Etha Collier, age eighteen, were all murdered in Mississippi. *The New York Times* of June 10, 1971, attributed the killings to "a general white fear of black political strength."

But through the efforts of the federal government and, more importantly, the people, the rural vigilantism of the South is being defeated. And it was the rural areas where the black right to vote was most seriously repressed. Now black candidates are being voted in by large blocs of voters who are no longer afraid to take advantage of their constitutional rights.

The victory of freedom over vigilantism is always encouraging. A lessening of rural vigilantism in general seems inevitable because there is a steady decline in the amount of rural land. More and more people are building homes on what was formerly farmland. With these settlers a broader mental horizon and new ideas will become more dominant. But as the countryside gives birth to new surburban areas, the problem of suburban vigilantism may develop and grow in seriousness and scope.

8

Today:
Suburban Vigilantes

Suburbia is a twentieth-century invention created to supply an environment for those people who wanted to escape urban living and reside in a country-like atmosphere. The emigrants were not ready to be weaned totally from city life so they sought homes where they could have a plot of grass and a few trees, yet still be near a city for work and entertainment. Starting in the late 1940s and continuing up to now, colonies of look-alike homes have sprung up in potato fields, Florida swamps, rolling midwest farms, and brown California hills.

The homes into which these city dwellers moved were not very different from the apartments they had been so eager to leave. Built on plots measuring 60 × 100 feet or 80 × 100 feet, the houses were so close together that they probably would have made a rural resident claustrophobic. Yet these green patches seemed large to the newcomers when compared to the close-packed city streets they had left behind.

The instant towns of suburbia became known as "bedroom communities" because the men worked in the city and only came home at night. The popularity of these suburban settings rested on the fact that there had been a wartime baby boom and the newlyweds wanted to escape such city problems as poor schooling, rising crime, and the increasing nonwhite population. Privately, many people felt the last problem was responsible for the first two. The families who fled the city were usually second- or third-generation Americans in their twenties or early thirties and nouveau middle class. Suburban values, therefore, became middle class and mostly Republican.

The Promised Land, however, had its drawbacks. The main one was economic. Unexpected costs ambushed the naive suburbanite. Transportation was costly. The new communities lacked mass-transportation systems so a car was needed and, in some cases, two or more per family. Insurance, upkeep, and gasoline siphoned a considerable part of Dad's paycheck. Also, the suburban communities had grown so fast that no educational provisions existed for the unexpected rise in school populations. The cost of extensive school busing and building construction was reflected in stampeding school taxes.

Worse, there were psychological problems. Suburbia is a melting pot of sorts. Though these new villages were predominantly white, there was a racial and religious mixture. In the city the families had usually lived in sections composed of their own ethnic background. A man might work with a wide variety of people, but at home he was surrounded by his own kind. But now a person's neighbors could be of many national origins. If an argument developed between two neighbors, the cause was usually blamed on the other person's ethnic background. Civic matters such as school board elections were affected by racial or religious bloc votes.

Family life changed drastically because grandparents and other relatives were miles away and had little influence on the maturing children. Family ties were noticeably weaker in the new generation. Other pressures often brought on devastating neuroses: "Keeping up with the Joneses" or the husband's frantic drive for business success or using a child's social or scholastic achievements to establish neighborhood superiority.

The irony, however, was that even before the twenty-year mortgages were paid off, the city problems that everyone had fled caught the 5:02 commuter express from the city and moved in next door. Schools and communities had trouble with juvenile gangs. Vandals smashed picture windows and invaded outdoor parties. House break-ins swept suburbia. And the bitterest irony of all for the first settlers of suburbia: More and more blacks and Mexican-Americans and Puerto Ricans were able to make the down payment on a home and join the exodus from urban strife.

Perhaps because the motivation for the move from cities was an escape from these very situations, suburban vigilantism most often arises to counteract these problems. In a way the cause of suburban vigilantism is a throwback to the basic impetus for vigilantism in America wherein the colonies treated harshly anyone who threatened their reason for fleeing to the colonies or venturing westward.

One of the dangers suburbanites wished to escape in their move from the cities was the drug problem. At first suburbanites felt safe from this scourge. Too late they learned no one, anywhere, was safe.

Wyandanch, New York, is such a suburban town. In 1940 the land was made up of farms. By 1970 Wyandanch had become a large residential area, populated mainly by blacks. Though there were many well-kept homes in Wyandanch, there were also houses with peeling paint and debris-littered lawns. The shopping centers had clusters of loitering youths, walls decorated with spray-painted obscenities, and a prosperous drug trade.

Thirty minutes away from Wyandanch is C. W. Post College set on the hilly grounds of an old Brookville estate. The college has tree-shaded walks, a mixture of old and new architecture, and a prosperous drug trade. A November 1971 editorial in the C. W. Post *Pioneer* stated that "heroin can be obtained as easily as cigarettes anywhere on campus." Despite a similarity in drug problems, Wyandanch and C. W. Post do not usually have the same inhabitants.

One Wyandanch mother was determined that her son would make the move from Wyandanch to C. W. Post. Catherine Young saw to it that her son Daryl was well motivated throughout his school years. He was graduated from high school with an A average and was the recipient of a Martin Luther King Scholarship to C. W. Post, which, according to Mrs. Young, Daryl considered a big step in his life.

One night in October 1971, Mrs. Young received a phone call from Daryl who was at C. W. Post. "Mom, you got me off the streets of Wyandanch, but it's worse here. Mama, you can get hooked here for free."

On Saturday, October 30, Daryl went to Manhattan with a college friend. Three days later Daryl Young's body was identified at the Bellevue morgue. The cause of death: cyanide-laced heroin. Daryl had been found, lying face down in a tenement doorway at 315 West 120th Street. Abandoned by his friend, the eighteen-year-old boy had had his clothes and valuables stolen. Reactions to the boy's death were filled with grief, fear, and anger.

Mrs. Young hoped that in some way Daryl's death would serve as a warning. She prayed that "some other mother would be spared the agony of sending her son's best suit to the funeral parlor, so he can be buried properly."

The director of security for the college, George Sutton, emphatically stated, "Anyone we catch selling heroin and other hard drugs on this campus will leave this campus in chains."

Irate Brookville students were skeptical about the effectiveness of the college's security force. Susan Sporn, a student, wrote to the *Pioneer* demanding that the security forces expend less energy towing away illegally parked automobiles and do something about a knifing on the campus and the "innumerable rapes and robberies in the dorms."

Another student writing to the *Pioneer* was more violent:

> Dear Editor:
> It seems to me that after two deaths due to drug overdose at C. W. Post, something would be done to rid ourselves of the short, red-haired dope pusher who is successfully hooking a number of students in our dormitory community. In Harlem responsible citizens are pushing creeps like this off rooftops.
>
> Anonymous

Other C. W. Post students felt as strongly as the anonymous letter writer, so an unofficial band of vigilantes began watching for pushers of hard drugs. If a seller had been spotted, he would have been accosted by a gang of male students within minutes. For several weeks the mood was tense on the Brookville campus though no one is quite sure exactly what would have happened if the vigilantes had captured a pusher. One student explained, "Word was out that it would be very unhealthy for a city pusher to be found around Post."

The vigilantes never apprehended a victim, which, knowing the high rate of injustice connected with vigilantism, may have been just as well. No one left the campus in chains. No one pushed the short, red-haired dope pusher off a rooftop. And the same student who was there when the vigilantes were keeping their fruitless watch admitted that today heroin is still as easy to obtain as cigarettes. So in this instance vigilantism failed and the problem continued.

No one can be surprised that the vigilantes had so

little success. The students' reaction to the drug deaths was right. The defense they selected to prevent further tragedies was wrong. Why, in the 1970s, would anyone use a weapon that is almost two hundred years old and that was faulty when it was first produced? Even the target was ill-chosen. The pusher only serves the customer. Admittedly, many pushers create their market by first offering drugs free to hook the customer, which may be what Daryl was referring to in the phone call to his mother. The real villain, however, is the drug culture.

Suburban vigilantism frequently erupts, too, when members of a different ethnic or religious group attempt to move into a hitherto all-white, Christian neighborhood. The first efforts of suburban residents to prevent such intrusions were subtle, but usually effective. House sellers would tell any blacks or Jews who came to inspect the property that it had already been sold, or else they would raise the price to one disproportionate to the value of the property. Real estate agents knew those communities which wished to remain all white and discreetly steered nonwhites into other areas. If someone did sell a house to a Jewish or black family, painted warnings like "Nigger, Keep Out!" or giant swastikas were smeared across the walls. Or the ultimate method of suburban vigilantes was employed: arson.

Vigilantism of this type went underground after most states passed antidiscrimination laws. These laws enable state civil rights commissions to bring charges against real estate brokers or any other sellers or renters of real property discovered engaging in discriminatory tactics in their business practices. The underground vigilantes relied mostly on terrorist attacks to drive the unwanted families away, but there were still some vigilantes who attempted more open, direct methods.

Essex Fells is a northern New Jersey community of about three thousand all-white inhabitants. Mr. and Mrs. Christian Heidt put their Essex Fells house on the market for $75,000 and found a buyer. A Newark lawyer, Myron S. Lehman, thought the area and especially the eleven-room ranch house was perfect for himself, his wife Doris, and their two children. The Heidts and Lehmans signed a sale contract for the agreed price. On the adjoining property lived John C. McDonough, the forty-three-year-old president of R. A. McDonough Company, one of the biggest northern New Jersey tire dealers. He, too, was a comparatively new resident of Essex Fells, having moved there from South Orange, New Jersey.

According to information from a state civil rights worker, McDonough raised "holy hell in the neighborhood" in an effort to block the sale to the Lehmans, who are Jews. Mr. Lehman claimed he wanted to arrange an interview with McDonough in an attempt to settle the problem, but McDonough refused. McDonough allegedly said on the phone, "I moved from South Orange to get away from your kind of people." Also, claimed Lehman, McDonough issued veiled threats when he said that Mr. Lehman would find it very difficult living in Essex Fells as would Lehman's wife and the six- and eight-year-old children.

Though the Lehmans and Heidts cancelled their sales contract and the Lehmans subsequently bought an $85,-000 home in Short Hills, New Jersey, the incident was not forgotten. The New Jersey State Division on Civil Rights was informed about the circumstances and brought charges against McDonough. The division holds the weight of a grand jury, and its findings are enforceable by the courts.

The conviction would have been the first time someone in New Jersey not directly involved with a house sale had been found guilty of discrimination. As a result McDonough could be forced to make good the additional $10,000 the Lehmans paid for their Short Hills home as well as the fees lost by the real estate broker and the lawyers involved in the Heidts' sale.

While the case was waiting to be heard by the Civil Rights Division, the New Jersey Anti-Defamation League of B'nai B'rith stated that McDonough ought to resign his governor-appointed position as the Legalized Games of Chance Control Commissioner. The post, which McDonough received in 1965 for a five-year term, determines whether or not there has been any violation of state laws dealing with bingo and raffles. McDonough refused to answer the demands.

On August 16, 1968, the Director of the Division on Civil Rights found John C. McDonough guilty and ordered him to "henceforth Cease and Desist from directly, indirectly, or in any manner, fashion, or form engaging in conduct amounting to such unlawful discrimination." No fines or punishment were imposed and

McDonough did not appeal the decision.

McDonough did claim, "I've been accused of thinking and saying things I didn't think or say."

Here, then, was a case when an official organization stepped in to protect the rights of an individual threatened by vigilantism.

Outbursts of vigilantism can also arise when people feel their rights are not being preserved by authorized groups. A situation somewhere between vigilantism and legal community action took place in Roosevelt, New York, a predominantly black suburb in Long Island's Nassau county, about thirty miles from New York City.

On the night of November 27, 1971, two blacks stole an automobile in nearby Lynbrook. The Nassau county police chased the stolen car for six miles during which the driver tried to run down a policeman. When the car reached Roosevelt, the driver slammed on the brakes. Two occupants fled on foot. Patrolman Frank Parisi chased a black youth who he claimed had jumped from the stolen automobile. Sixteen-year-old Larry Blaycock stopped running and wheeled about toward the policeman. At this point Patrolman Parisi thought the boy meant to shoot him so he fired his service revolver once. Blaycock died. The driver was never apprehended.

The black community became aroused when it heard about the death of the unarmed youth, who, it was learned, had been mentally retarded. A Nassau county grand jury of twenty-two whites and one black found Patrolman Parisi innocent of any charges. The streets and homes of Roosevelt were filled with angry discussions of the robbery and the shooting. Fearing further violence, black leaders of the community devised a means to alleviate the tension. The plan was carefully worked out because the leaders realized that if their plan was not handled well, terrible complications might result.

Church and civil leaders knew that community anger focused on two aspects of the situation: 1) the shooting itself and 2) the grand jury's findings. (There was strong community feeling that the grand jury, which had contained only one black member, had been prejudiced in favor of the white policeman.) The leaders decided to allow the people in Roosevelt to hold their own trial with the defendant in absentia. Twelve days after the shooting, the hour-long mock trial was conducted by a judge, a twelve-man jury, a prosecutor, and two defense attorneys. The twenty-four people involved were black teenagers or young adults.

The defense lawyers argued that the black youth had "signed his own death warrant when he turned as if to shoot."

The prosecutor, who only identified himself as "Brother David," summed up his case by declaring, "We do not need mad dogs running amok in our community under the name of 'law and order.' We are not dogs. We will not be treated as dogs."

While the jury deliberated, the Rev. Robert C. Champan, a Roosevelt resident who is the executive director of the department of social injustice of the National Council of Churches, spoke to the one hundred spectators. "We are talking to the community and not the whites. The whites won't listen." He went on to say killing the mentally retarded Blaycock represented "an American kind of justice that has demanded a life for a car."

The verdict was guilty.

Investigating the psychology of the community meeting reveals benefits as well as possible dangers. When people are not allowed to voice their feelings in some recognizable fashion, their frustration and anger build to a point where they may erupt in violence. The church-run "trial" permitted an opportunity to release pent-up opinions and gave residents of the community a sense that someone was listening. Possibly the ones who were in attendance were not those who could effect a change, but an audience is an audience, nevertheless. When the guilty verdict was handed down, an ersatz punishment had been inflicted on the person they all considered guilty. Some people therefore must have experienced a sense of closure about the Parisi case. These individuals would then be less likely to engage in more violent activities. But there are aspects of the situation that make one wonder if the mock trial might not have led to more militant action.

The tribunal gave Parisi an undefined "sentence" that would be carried out at the "people's convenience." The very wording conjures up an image of corporal punishment inflicted by guerrilla attack. Possibly the sentence was not spelled out because the organizers of the meeting intended to register a legal protest or complaint through authorized channels and did not want to tip their hand ahead of time. Or, perhaps, the intent of the trial was to wage psychological warfare on the police, hoping to make them less prone to shoot fleeing suspects in the future. But the wording could have encouraged some young blacks to go further than the trial, much as the SAO literature inspired someone to shoot at Professor Bohmer's house in San Diego.

Following the mock trial one youth said, "It's a start. It won't stop here."

The question which then comes to mind is the same one that may be asked of any form of vigilantism. Where *will* it stop?

Thankfully, the Roosevelt mock trial did not give birth to further violence. The temper of the community did cool off. Therefore the church leaders must have had firm control of all the factors. Yet the scheme was a dangerous one. In less able hands an incident of full-fledged vigilantism might have occurred.

In most cases the anger and the desire to correct an unpleasant situation are well-founded. If all energy and talent were channeled into a fight against the right problem in the best way, the struggle might very well be successful. Suburban vigilantism, like its older and younger siblings, always seems the easiest way and is initially the most satisfying because it affords the participants a chance to feel they are doing something. Rarely, however, if ever, is vigilantism the wisest approach to the problem of law enforcement in any community.

9

Today:

Urban Vigilantes

Nowhere today is the climate of fear as oppressive as in American cities. Any urban gathering has discussions detailing personal experiences or tales of friends who were involved in purse snatchings, apartment break-ins, or assaults. People carry tear gas spray tubes or mace in their pockets. Single women can buy life-size inflatible rubber men so there will seem to be another person in their car or home. In the following excerpts, there is an underlying theme as well as an overt similarity.

LETTER: "Be sure to go there. It's not in the nicest section of London. But don't worry. It's not New York City so you won't get mugged."

CONVERSATION: "You get the best buys in the city shops, you know. But no one goes into Baltimore. If

you park your car, you come back and find it rifled.
They do have parking garages. But thugs assault you
on the various levels. There are security guards with
dogs, but they can't be everywhere at once, you know."

CONVERSATION: "Did you know that all along the
streets of Detroit there are signs telling you to keep
your car doors locked and windows rolled up. And
these signs are put up by the city?"

PHONE CALL: "Is there any other way to get there?
Taking a bus means going into the city. And with the
way New York is these days we don't want to do that!"

With urban crime soaring, the amount of urban
vigilantism is also climbing, as bands of citizens form
community protection groups. Springfield, Massachusetts, has the Crimewatch where unarmed volunteers
patrol in pairs with walkie-talkies. If they encounter any
crime, they may intervene or call for assistance from the
police. The New Jersey Civil Mobile Patrol, Inc., has
forty members and thirty mobile units. In a letter dis-
seminating information to state communities, they describe their activities as "reporting accidents and fires,
helping disabled cars, trying to locate children missing
from their homes, reporting gang fights." They also keep
a sharp watch for thieves and vandals as the mobile unit
cruises the streets. Volunteer police forces such as the
Civil Mobile Patrol are in reality vigilantes though they
are not a danger because they are under tight supervision from within and by official police departments.

But there are urban vigilantes who are loosely structured and, therefore, more liable to commit excesses.

WHO KILLED THE 10 DRUG PUSHERS? asked a *New York Times* headline in January 1972. The answer was provided in the subhead: "Some Say Vigilantes Among Minorities Murdered Them."

Urban ghettos have been the hardest-hit sections when it comes to the sale of hard drugs. Worse, little seems to be done about it. Residents feel that the police are ignoring the problem or, at best, making token arrests. Police say they get no support from the community and that for every addict arrested, many more rise up to take his or her place. Pushers openly ply their trade, entering elementary, junior high, and senior high schools.

"I never gave a thought whether it was right or wrong. It was just a way of making money," a former Harlem pusher said. His weekly profit had been between $4,000 and $5,000.

Ghetto inhabitants have given a great deal of thought to the problem and have decided something must be done to drive the pushers out of the area. As far as these residents are concerned, the pushers are selling death, so that is what the pusher gets if he does not move on. That apparently was the choice offered to drug sellers in Brower Park in Bedford-Stuyvesant, a section of Brooklyn, New York, named for the Duke of Bedford and Peter Stuyvesant. Ninety per cent of Bedford-Stuyvesant's population is black, and its problems are monumental: drug addiction, high school dropouts, broken families, jobless men, rotting buildings, and the highest infant mortality rate in the United States. The residents of Bedford-Stuyvesant in the early 1970s were eking out a bitter day-to-day existence, awaiting salvation or death. But many had no intention of receiving death in small plastic envelopes from some pusher who was living the good life somewhere else.

Brower Park, bordered by Prospect Avenue, Park Place, and Kingston Avenue, was little used by the people living in the area. Undesirables of every manner made the park their meeting place and were responsible for many threats and assaults on the decent citizens.

In July 1972 a sudden change occurred.

Bedford-Stuyvesant residents compared the events to "cowboy movies on TV": men with guns hid behind trees and bushes; shots echoed up the streets lined with brownstone tenements; police sirens screamed in the distance; some people ran, others gathered. Over a period of eighteen months there were ten unsolved murders and numerous shootings of persons *suspected* of narcotics distribution.

Today? "The muggings have ceased, and the break-ins are fewer. It's cleared up beautifully in the park—the neighborhood people use the park again." So said Mrs. Julia Beadenkopf, vice president of the Sterling Park and Kingston Block Association. Women in the area agreed with her, adding that much of the narcotics traffic has moved away.

Not so, claimed Detective Padraic Nugent of the 77th Precinct in Brooklyn. "I have not been cognizant of either an increase or decrease in the sale of hard drugs in the area."

Black youths living around Brower Park, however, informed a *New York Times* reporter that drug sales in the neighborhood had declined considerably because "the brothers did a thing." Though these teenagers did not specify who the "brothers" were, other youths said that the shootings were the work of a "family" of members from several gangs. The purpose, one boy explained, was "to push all the addicts, pushers, and faggots out of this park."

If the shootings and murders in Bedford-Stuyvesant were the work of outlaw, urban vigilantes, there are other city-based organizations that keep constant and effective guard against the inroads of vigilantism. Harold Jones, chief of the Mayor's Office of Neighborhood Government in New York City, estimated that there were more than four thousand block associations in the entire city.

"You name it," he said in May 1972, "and there's a block association doing something about it. Sprucing up the area, narcotics, baby-sitting, art classes, hockey leagues, patrols, stop signs, parties, repaving. . . ."

One particularly effective group that has been "doing something about" their area is the Jane Street Block Association. Jane Street is five blocks long, starting at the chic boutiques of Greenwich Avenue in New York City and ending in the grimy pier section under the West Side Highway. Along the way there are elegant townhouses, crumbling brownstones, and the historical residence of Alexander Hamilton. Twenty-five hundred people call Jane Street home.

Though Jane Street was not plagued with unusual

problems, the section did have its share of urban blight. Late in 1970 thirty citizens gathered in a townhouse to discuss how to clean up Jane Street. Their immediate concerns were varied. No Sanitation Department crew seemed disposed to remove the bedspring that lay in the middle of the street. Trees and shrubbery were scarce. Paper and garbage littered the pavements. Heavy trailer trucks raced along the street, their drivers uncaring about traffic laws or the safety of children. Thievery and burglary were everyday occurrences. An assorted collection of derelicts, panhandlers, addicts, and muggers staggered along the sidewalk or hovered in doorways.

The newly formed Jane Street Block Association followed set procedures and worked through the mayor's office. Shortly after the group had formed and the first phone calls were made, the rusting bedspring disappeared. Even when private guards were hired to patrol the five-block stretch, liaison men for the association sought police cooperation. No trigger-happy vigilante was going to be seen along Jane Street if the association had its way. The private guards have no firearms, each guard's only weapon being a club. Each also carries handcuffs and a walkie-talkie. The guards are also without the authority to arrest and may only detain a suspect until the police arrive. Sixteen hours a day the men criss-cross every fifteen minutes as they help to prevent crime and assist residents or visitors.

Both the inhabitants of the Jane Street area and the police have greeted the guards with enthusiasm. Recently, when some members of the association were collecting funds to help pay for the guards, one donor waxed ecstatic: "Let me tell you, I'm very pleased. Before the guards, Jane Street used to be full of panhandlers and drunks and beggars. Now I see hardly any."

The commander of the local police precinct added his support: "In fact we *welcome* the guards. The block associations are doing a terrific job. They're our eyes and ears on the street, and we appreciate it."

Everyone values the work of the Jane Street Block Association and their hired patrols. No one can estimate the amount of crime that has been eliminated though a clue may lie in the results of January 1972. In that month alone, the patrols chased away twelve car thieves, prowlers, and loiterers and cornered one mugger, and all this was done with no danger to innocent citizens and with no one's rights being overruled, because the Jane Street Association carefully toes the line between legal community action and vigilantism.

Another figure who also appears to toe that line, though he or she most frequently ascends to power as crime and disorder rise, is the politician who makes "law and order" his or her campaign promise. Not all such men and women should be accused of hypocrisy or opportunism, for many may sincerely believe they can help alleviate the conditions that are hurting their constituents. But in their attempt to make themselves in effect the elected leaders of a vigilante band, all such politicians capitalize on the emotionalism that surrounds the rising crime rate.

The causes of the crime rate are diverse, and no simplistic solution is available. Politicians who promise to provide their supporters with quick results, may have to resort to actions that, like those of vigilantes, infringe upon people's rights. All American voters realize they should investigate a candidate's promises and background and potentialities. What is the person offering to do while in office? Is it feasible? Does the individual possess the means to expedite his or her goals? Or is the candidate trying to color the campaign with emotional issues that will blind people and make the voters react with feelings rather than with intelligence?

Consider the time and place and audience of this political statement.

The 1964 Republican Convention met in San Francisco's Cow Palace to nominate presidential and vice-presidential candidates. No doubt really existed that Senator Barry Goldwater from Arizona would be the choice. His important victory in the California primary as well as the thorough groundwork of his local, county, and state followers made the decision practically a formality.

This was the year that conservatism ruled the Republican Convention. A platform amendment to condemn extremism and the Ku Klux Klan was booed and voted down. Senator Goldwater's main hope of beating Lyndon Johnson was the support of a southern electorate that was thoroughly displeased with civil rights legislation and the help that the southern blacks were getting to achieve their rights.

Senator Goldwater stepped before this body that had vocally supported the Klan and that represented many citizens who believed the Klan heritage to be an honorable one. The presidential candidate told his audience that extremism in the defense of liberty was no vice and that moderation in the pursuit of justice was no virtue. Though Goldwater later formally announced that he did not want Klan support, his afterthoughts failed to convince many people, least of all Klan members. Robert Creel, Alabama Klan Dragon, addressed a rural Alabama meeting about Senator Goldwater and about George Wallace, who was then running for governor. Creel announced, "They need our help!"

This then is the danger of a politician whose emotional values are similar to those of the vigilante. Almost inevitably such a politician attracts the support of people who believe in a vigilante solution to problems like crime and law enforcement.

One such political campaign took place in Philadelphia during the fall of 1971. The major decision to be reached that year was the choosing of a mayor. The man elected to such an important position must handle a variety of responsibilities. Unfortunately the problem of law and order so dominated the Philadelphia mayoralty campaign that little else was discussed by the candidates or newspapers.

One Philadelphia resident described the situation this way: "The rising crime rate, danger on the streets, people afraid to go out at night, downtown overrun by hippies and hoodlums, the drug problem, graffiti wherever one looked, all created a mood of exasperation." What this resident did not say was that there existed a widespread belief, particularly among middle- and lower-class whites, that the problems were caused by the blacks. The man who supported that theory and appeared able to do something to eliminate the problems was virtually assured of this bloc vote.

Two candidates were offered to the people. The minority Republican party put up fifty-year-old Thatcher Longstreth, a Quaker from Main Line Philadelphia. Six feet six inches tall—he had made "All-American" at Princeton—Longstreth was a city councilman and the former executive director of the Chamber of Commerce. Politically he might be labeled moderately liberal.

Opposing Longstreth was Democrat Frank Rizzo, a high school dropout. Rizzo called himself the "toughest cop in America," and he had twenty-eight years on the police force to prove it. For the last four years he had been Philadelphia's police commissioner. With Democratic voters outnumbering Republicans two to one, Rizzo was the favored man from the start. Even so the political sparring was vigorous and never veered from the question of race and crime; the favorite topic of conversation of today's urban vigilantes.

"The streets will be made safe," said Supercop Rizzo.

"Rizzo was a helluva tough cop," stated City Councilman Tom M. Foglietta, a Republican. "He could bash more heads in faster than any ten men I know. But Philadelphia needs more than a tough cop. It does not need a mayor who has to use threats to get things done."

Throughout the city huge billboards were plastered with "Rizzo Means Business." Democrats claimed this was an attempt to show the Republican businessmen that Rizzo had their interests at heart. Others countered by explaining the phrase was meant to impress people that Rizzo was going to get tough with blacks. An incident that had occurred while Rizzo was police commissioner was used to depict the type of treatment blacks might expect under a Rizzo regime. A group of Black Panthers suspected of carrying concealed weapons were arrested, herded into the street, and stripped. Many people felt that the police could have searched the suspects without subjecting them to public humiliation.

The Rev. Leon H. Sullivan, the first black member of the General Motors Board of Directors and founder of a national job-training program called Opportunities Industrialization Center, was strongly against Rizzo. "Both Mr. Rizzo and Mr. Longstreth are for law and order, as we all are, but it is a question of law and order and progress under Longstreth or law and order and terror under Rizzo."

Rizzo campaigned in the working-class, white areas, avoiding black ghettos. Former Philadelphia Mayor Richardson Dillworth accused Rizzo of telling voters in off-the-record meetings that "I'm the guy who can keep the blacks in their place." Rizzo's opponent, Longstreth, who was endorsed by liberals of both parties, spoke in black neighborhoods and white neighborhoods as well as in poor sections and rich sections of Philadelphia.

Two weeks before election, *The New York Times* reported that Longstreth was gaining on his opponent. A group of Democrats defected and formed the New Democratic Coalition of Philadelphia, endorsing Longstreth. They called their decision a repudiation of everything Frank Rizzo stood for—"the politics of racism and the politics of fear."

On Election night when 1,749 of 1,755 voting precincts counted their ballots, there were 343,204 votes for Longstreth and 391,239 for Rizzo. Fear had won. The balloting had followed racial rather than traditional party lines. Longstreth had done well in black areas and Rizzo had captured the working-class whites.

The Philadelphia *Bulletin* said: "When crime and street violence is commonplace, it is not surprising that some people will turn to a man who became the symbol of law and order."

And so it is with any form of vigilantism. When conditions frighten urban dwellers, they must constantly be aware of where their fear may lead them. Individually or collectively, they may be attracted to some person or some group who seems able to protect them and to defend them against the danger. Too late they may find they have turned not to an avenue that will lead them to better conditions, but to illegal suppression.

10

Today: Political, Racial, and Religious Vigilantes

Christmas 1971 was a particularly important season for downtown merchants in Cleveland, Ohio. Their businesses had fallen off badly ever since people had begun avoiding the central city business area and going instead to suburban shopping centers. In preparation for the 1971 Christmas shopping weeks, the worried downtown businessmen had put up $50,000 for free bus rides. Any customer who would come downtown to shop could ride free. The gimmick was very successful. Shoppers, overcoming their fear of crime and racial animosity, began arriving downtown in hordes.

On Tuesday evening, December 21, Anita Howard told her husband that they should take advantage of the free bus ride so their three sons could enjoy seeing Santa Claus. The Howards lived in Glenwood, a black neighborhood on Cleveland's East Side. At first Tyrone

Howard refused, but when his wife insisted, "If you don't come with me, I'll take the kids myself," the entire Howard family left Glenwood, bound for Higbee's Department Store.

On the same Tuesday evening Mr. and Mrs. John Fitzpatrick and their four children also traveled downtown to Higbee's so the children could see Santa Claus. However, they came in their car, not on the free bus. The Fitzpatricks were celebrating a special Christmas, for it was to be their last in their old home in the Cleveland suburb of Euclid. Their new house on the West Side would be completed early in 1972.

Tyrone Howard and John Fitzpatrick met on the tenth floor of the store. According to witnesses, Fitzpatrick was already on the Santa Claus line when Howard pushed in ahead. The wait had been long and many of the parents had put in a full day's work. Fitzpatrick accused Howard of cutting into line, saying something like, "That's a cheap trick" or "This irks the hell out of me." No one was quite sure. Howard, in return, denied he had acted unfairly, but it was reported he uttered some obscenities and that Fitzpatrick then told Howard not to use that kind of talk in front of children.

The argument became more heated. Anita Howard claimed another man urged her husband on by saying, "Are you going to let that honky talk to you like that?" But no one else appeared to notice that person.

Within moments Fitzpatrick and Howard were punching and kicking each other. Then John Fitzpatrick crumpled to the floor, dying from knife wounds.

The New York Times reported: "Judging by the time and the words it appeared to be a Christmas crime— the kind that comes when men are tired and touchy— and also a racial crime, the kind that happens when men from different racial worlds meet." The newspaper might have added that the senseless killing was also an example of individual vigilantism—the kind that occurs when an individual believes that his or her freedom and desires are the only ones that are valid.

Five months later and in a different section of the United States Alabama's Governor George A. Wallace stepped up to his bullet-proof podium. The weather in Laurel, Maryland, was sultry, more like midsummer than May 16, but the one thousand or so people were attentive while the Alabaman spoke. The eighty-eight-store shopping center, shaped like a huge U, held the red, white, and blue speaker's platform in its cup. At the conclusion of his talk, Wallace shed his coat and stepped down to meet his admirers. As he shook hands, a man's voice from Wallace's left repeatedly called, "Hey, George, come over here. Hey, George." Wallace veered left, stopping to shake hands with Mrs. Brigitte Howkins of Hyattsville, Maryland.

"Good luck, Governor Wallace," she said, possibly referring to the Maryland primary, which was to be held the next day.

Mrs. Howkins later told reporters, "He smiled at me, dropped my hand, and reached out for another when the man who had been standing on my right lifted his right arm, and suddenly there were shots."

Wallace toppled backward, arms akimbo. Four or five Prince Georges county police dove for the alleged assailant. They dragged him from the crowd as people shouted, "Get him. Get that bastard." Mrs. Wallace comforted her husband while they waited for the ambulance that would take him to Holy Cross Hospital in Silver Springs. Blood from chest, stomach, and arm wounds stained Wallace's blue shirt.

Karen Yengish, a reporter for the Laurel *News Leader* later said, "I never thought I would see anything like this, especially in Laurel. It's a small community. It's probably Wallace country. I mean, it's middle America."

The foregoing incidents are just two examples of the acts of vigilantism that probably frighten people most today: the incomprehensible, useless, unexpected, stabbings, shootings, and bombings. The country seems overrun with individuals who, at the slightest provocation, use the most violent means to attack what they do not like. There are countless other examples.

Each of the twenty congressmen who had voted against an appropriation to the House Committee on Un-American Activities, therefore displeasing the far-Right Minutemen, received the following warning letter:

> See the old man at the corner where you buy your paper? He may have a silencer equipped pistol under his coat. That extra fountain pen of the insurance salesman who calls on you might be a cyanide gas gun. What about your milkman? Arsenic works slow but sure. Your auto mechanic may stay up nights studying booby traps. These patriots are not going to let you

take away their freedom from them. They have learned
the silent knife, the strangler's cord, the target rifle
that hits the sparrows at 200 yards. Traitors beware!
Even now the cross hairs are on the back of your necks.

What many people may not realize is that the senseless attacks on people or institutions that are reported
daily in the news media are examples of vigilantism.
And when citizens form groups to fight back, they are
creating counter-vigilante mobs, which history has shown
only intensifies the violence. Counter-vigilante bands,
whether the Moderators of colonial South Carolina or
modern-day gangs, can become as dangerous as the
vigilantism they pledge themselves to fight. One such
counter-vigilante group was organized in Brooklyn, New
York, to protect its members and their friends or relatives.

In 1968 the ghetto schools in New York City were in
trouble. Not with student discipline, which was a perpetual problem, but with adult blacks who wanted more
voice in their children's education. Several schools were
subjected daily to shouting men and women. To provide protection for the Jewish teachers who worked in
these schools each day, Rabbi Meir Kahane formed the
Jewish Defense League. JDL members escorted the
teachers to the buildings while angry blacks milled
around them. The league assumed other defensive
duties. Many Jewish residents were assaulted by black
youths on Brooklyn streets. JDL patrols, armed with
baseball bats and billy clubs, walked the sidewalks
nightly. The beneficial effect of the guards was obvious.

Fewer attacks took place in the area.

Success can be heady, and so it was for the Jewish Defense League. Kahane and his followers decided to broaden the scope of their operations. In fact, they tackled one of the most powerful countries in the world, the U.S.S.R.

Twelve Russians were arrested in June 1970 and charged by a Soviet court with plotting to hijack an airplane. Ten of these supposed skypirates were Jews. Angered by what it considered persecution of fellow religionists, the Jewish Defense League declared war on the Soviet Union.

A synagogue across from the Soviet Mission in New York City was "liberated." The "liberation forces" of the JDL draped huge anti-Soviet banners across the face of the building and hooked up loudspeakers that blared martial music. The psychological warfare became a bit more militant when JDL members occupied the New York offices of Aeroflot, the Soviet airline, and Tass, news agency of the Soviet. Anti-Russian slogans were painted on a Soviet airliner at Kennedy Airport.

Kahane, a thirty-eight-year-old, lean, dynamic man with two law degrees, said, "When we started out . . . people told us we were a flea going up against an elephant. Well, the flea has grown pretty big."

Kahane was right. Russian diplomatic officials came from a country where spontaneous political demonstrations were not permitted. So even the pinprick bites of a flea were annoying. United States officials were worried about the effect on Soviet-American relations. Kahane dismissed the diplomacy between the two countries as "building bridges over Jewish bodies." A sign in JDL headquarters expressed the league's seriousness: "2 Russians for every Jew."

In January 1971 a lead-pipe bomb exploded outside the yellow brick Soviet Embassy Cultural Annex in Washington, D.C. Although no one was injured, the blast shattered windows and tore loose a fifty-pound courtyard door. Thirty minutes later an anonymous phone call was received by the Washington bureau of the Associated Press. "This is a sample of things to come," said the female voice. "Let our people go. Never again!"

"Never Again" appears on the JDL button along with a raised, clenched fist. The phrase refers to the Nazi slaughter of six million Jews. Younger, more militant Jews of today partly blame the Jews' own passivity for the inhuman treatment. "Never again," insists the JDL, will Jews sit back and allow themselves to be so mistreated.

Kahane was arrested, for the eleventh time, in January 1971 for rioting and disorderly conduct. At the same time other JDL members were charged with giving false names when they purchased rifles. *Newsweek* magazine reported Kahane as saying, "If they think we are the kind of people who will be scared off by jail threats, then they just don't know the psyche of the modern militant Jew."

The JDL denied any responsibility for the Washington bombing, but the organization did not condemn the attack. Further guerrilla actions took place, but whether the JDL had actually planned them or whether the group had inspired others to vigilante action, is not too clear. There were scuffles with the police, mice were set loose in a Philadelphia theater where the Russian Moiseyev dance troupe was performing, and a bomb exploded at a Soviet tourist office.

Dr. Marvin S. Antelman, the New England director of the JDL, quit after the bombings. "They condone it," he said. "I agree with the aims of the organization, but I do question what constitutes responsible action. It's like creating a Frankenstein monster."

The B'nai B'rith condemned the JDL's tactics as "morally reprehensible and politically self-defeating."

The American Jewish Committee stated: "What the JDL has done is going to bring out a lot of psychopaths —both Jewish and non-Jewish."

A bagful of bricks and mortar smashed the plate-glass window of Aeroflot. Demands, such as *"Poshli domoi"* (Go home) and *"Svoboda Yevreyam"* (Freedom for Jews), were painted on Soviet buildings and offices. A firebomb exploded in the office of theatrical impresario Sol Hurok who had brought the Moiseyev dancers to America. One young woman receptionist was killed and six other people were injured as a result of that bombing. The eighty-three-year-old showman suffered smoke inhalation.

Rabbi Kahane was on a mission to Israel when the Hurok office was bombed. He denied that JDL had had any connection with the incident and labeled the perpetrators "insane." Kahane apparently had no guilt feelings that his organization might have triggered those unbalanced mentalities to set the device. In fact, he appeared perfectly self-satisfied with the U.S. organization he had fathered and announced he was thinking of settling in Israel permanently and establishing a *World Jewish Defense League*.

Meanwhile the JDL in America continued its activities. *Newsweek* magazine reported that "Kahane claims a membership of 10,000 around the country but 1,000 seems more likely." Karate classes for Jews of all ages and a JDL summer camp where children receive rifle training were several of the services offered the Jewish community by the JDL. Kahane considered such military preparations necessary in order to protect the Jews from a serious domestic threat, said *Time* magazine (January 25, 1972). The threat, as Kahane sees it, comes from black militancy and from "those white liberals eager to help blacks at the expense of Jews."

Across the bay from Brooklyn is New Jersey, where another individual can be found who has organized a vigilante band to protect his people: Tony Imperiale, gun-toting city councilman of Newark. Imperiale feels his people—Italian-Americans—need protection from "a dual system. One set of rules for the blacks, another for us."

Imperiale formed the North Ward Citizens Committee after the Newark riots of 1968. The group has its base in a cinder-block building that has a sign reading "Imperiale Country" hanging outside. Imperiale Country is all white. The group was set up to defend whites, its members dress in white and drive a white ambulance. The solidly built Imperiale can be seen nightly, clad in a spotless white uniform, open at the neck and with an American flag embroidered on one shoulder, speeding through Newark streets on errands. During an interview with Columnist Stewart Alsop in 1971, the vigilante ambulance first stopped at a home of a couple engaged in a heated argument. When Imperiale got them "straightened out," he went on to get a heart-attack victim to the nearest hospital. But the North Ward Citizens Committee is prepared for more violent action. Ovid Demaris wrote in *America the Violent* that the "group boasted it kept a secret arsenal and could obtain a tank and two helicopters whenever they became necessary in the defense of the city's whites."

Guns are being cleaned, oiled, and loaded on both sides of the color line. The Black Panthers first made national headlines when they marched, guns in hand and bandoliers of cartridges strapped across their chests, into the California General Assembly. The dramatic entrance was meant to impress everyone with the Panthers' stand on the question of private citizens being allowed to carry unconcealed, loaded guns within city limits. The law in that instance was in their favor, but the photographs on TV and in newspapers and magazines so frightened white Americans that they were ready to believe the worst of the group.

The Black Panther Party was born in Oakland, California, sometime in 1966. Bobby G. Seale and Huey P. Newton felt an organization should be created that would defend blacks against the police. They were joined by the more militant Eldridge Cleaver, who urged blacks to arm themselves and shoot their enemies. The party took its name from the symbol of a lunging black panther used by the black Lowndes County Freedom Party in Alabama. This is the only connection between the two parties. The aim of the Black Panther party—to help blacks get complete control over their lives—attracted many youngsters from big city slum areas. The party grew rapidly, but almost from its inception the Panthers were plagued by violence.

Five months after the dramatic Panther entrance in Sacramento, Huey Newton and another Panther, Gene McKinney, decided to celebrate the end of Newton's three-year probation. They were riding in a Volkswagen belonging to Newton's fiancée when Officer Frey of the Oakland police spotted the car. He checked the license number with a list carried in all scout cars and radioed headquarters: "It's a known Panther vehicle." The policeman stopped the Volkswagen.

Within minutes Newton was wounded and Officer Frey was dead.

At the trial Newton testified he and his friends were hunting for a place that served "soul" food when the policeman stopped them. Frey, Newton claimed, had called him a "nigger," roughed him up, and then shot him without provocation.

Officer Herbert Heanes, who had come to Frey's assistance, said that Newton had been the one to fire the first shot.

Several other facts came out during the testimony. Neither Frey's gun nor Newton's weapon was found.

Repeated witnesses testified that Frey was a racist who
had waged a personal vendetta against blacks.

After four days, the jury brought in a verdict of
voluntary manslaughter. Newton faced a two- to fifteen-
year prison sentence.* A few days later, two Oakland
policemen drove past Panther headquarters and fired
carbine rifles into the building. They were subsequently
dropped from the force, charged with drinking and
firing a gun into an inhabited dwelling.

Shoot-outs between police and Panthers soon erupted
all across the United States. Chattanooga; Houston;
Charlotte, North Carolina; New Orleans, Denver, Chicago, all were scenes of cop-Panther confrontations.
Often there were unanswered questions about the battles. Were the attacks warranted? Were the Panthers the
ones who opened fire first? Were all these skirmishes
part of a nationwide drive to eliminate, by killing if
necessary, all the Black Panthers?

More troubles kept the Panthers in the news. Panther
party co-founder Bobby Seale and Ericka Huggins, a
New Haven Panther, were put on trial for crimes related to the 1969 murder of a fellow Panther, but a
mistrial was declared when the jury was unable to reach
a verdict. David Hilliard, Panther minister of information, was sent to prison for threatening President Nixon's
life. Twenty-one members in New York City charged
with conspiracy to blow up buildings, bridges, and tun-
nels were acquitted. Eldridge Cleaver fled the country

* In May 1970 the California Court of Appeals overturned Newton's conviction on the ground that the judge had not given proper
instruction to the jury.

rather than return to jail for violating his parole on a 1958 conviction of rape and assault to commit murder. In early 1973 he was living in Algeria, working there with the international section of the Black Panther Party that supports his philosophy of open revolution.

Recently, Panther leaders in the U.S. claimed there had been a change in their methods. The August 20, 1972, *New York Times* article, "Panthers Exchanging Guns for Ballots," quoted Bobby Seale who was running for mayor of Oakland:

"It's about time we started getting things together," said Mr. Seale. Conducting voter registration drives and running for local office are "part of our new program of going into politics at the grass-roots level."

Reports from two dozen cities bear Mr. Seale out. Ericka Huggins, who had been on trial with Seale, is now an elected member of the Berkeley Community Development Council. The Panthers endorsed Shirley Chisholm for President in 1972 and contributed $1,000 to her campaign. The Rev. Cecil A. Williams, a Methodist minister in the San Francisco area, said that the Panthers "are forming political coalitions, and they are relating to black churches, the local N.A.A.C.P. and other civil rights organizations, as well as religious, civic, and social clubs in order to get support."

The change in Panther philosophy created a serious split with Eldridge Cleaver when the Newton-Seale contingent was unable to convince Cleaver to discard the revolutionary line in favor of more democratic procedures. Bernice Jones, communications secretary for the New York Cleaver group, wrote in a letter to followers:

"At this time I would also like to point out that we are not a civil rights group. We are not an integrationist group or a segregationist group. We do not relate to the N.A.A.C.P. or Urban League ideology nor a pie in sky idealism. *We are a revolutionary organization whose sole function is to wage revolution in America*." (Italics added.)

The struggle of the Black Panther Party to change from a vigilante organization to a group that works along legal lines to obtain its goals may have a great influence on the U.S. in the next few years. Will the Panthers be able to convince a public conditioned to an extremist reputation that this new swing is sincere? (The 1972 fiscal report of the FBI, released in August 1972, seemed unaware of the new trend in Panther tactics. The report said that seven hundred ten full-time members of the Black Panther Party were still to be considered "a dangerous threat to internal security.") Will the internal strife and warfare be overcome? Can the new emotion stand up against failure at the polls? If the answer in each case is no, the recently adopted philosophy may be discarded and a reunion might take place with the Cleaver forces. If the answers are yes, then other groups that now place faith in murder and bombings might join the swing to legal action.

Political, racial and religious activism today seems the most frightening form of vigilantism because the extremists in today's society appear most often to come from one of these three types of vigilante groups. Yet there are other vigilantes who quietly and unobtrusively are eroding our personal liberties. These are the pseudo-vigilantes who employ pressure and fear to force everyone to adhere to their particular moral, political, or philosophical beliefs.

11

Today:
Pseudo-Vigilantes

"The general attitudes expressed by people in authority with respect to dissent leads me to believe that vigilance is extraordinarily important." So said Bernard Wolfman, president of the Greater Philadelphia chapter of the American Civil Liberties Union in the February 28, 1972, Philadelphia *Bulletin*. Wolfman went on to explain: "Just in the past few weeks, you've seen a fireman denied his employment because of personal hair style . . ."

During an August 1972 interview in Los Angeles initiated by *Publisher's Weekly* magazine, Dr. Daniel Ellsberg said that publishers and editors "have to decide whether they are prepared to admit a major and very broad assault is being made on the First Amendment, the right to publish and the freedom of speech. . . ."

An editorial from a high school underground newspaper in Nebraska gave this advice:

HIRAM IS LEGAL

The school administration has said that they will take away all copies of the paper, and they will suspend all students caught with one. This is a bluff and lie. It is meant to scare us into silence and you into ignorance. It is also illegal. . . .

No one has the authority to take away your property without due process (of law).

The principal does not have this power. He might think he has. So the next time he hassles you, set him right. Teach the teachers.

If a teacher says, "Give me that," say, "No! This is my personal property." Put the paper in your pocket. But know enough about your rights to speak intelligently about them.

—*Hiram*
Omaha, Nebraska

Not only being able to speak intelligently about your rights is important. The ability to defend your rights legally is vital today, for there are numerous attacks on the basic, democratic liberties of the ordinary citizen. The three quotes given above indicate an awareness by people of many different ages and backgrounds that groups do exist that would like to deprive individuals of their rights. The reasons for the attacks may be political or economic or philosophical, but whatever they are, the same purpose is there: a desire to make everyone conform to the particular vigilante group's belief.

As the editors of *Hiram,* an underground paper,

learned, many teachers, administrators, boards of education, and alumni associations will permit nothing to
change an educational institution into something they
personally are not prepared to accept. Dr. Kenneth
Kramer, chairman of the psychology department at
Trinity University, told the San Antonio *Daily News* in
February 1972 that this attitude is caused by fear. "It's
the fear of undermining their authority," he said. "They
are more concerned about control in the classroom than
encouraging debate [and] in educating the individual to
be free and critical." He added, "Anything that smacks
of independence has to be stopped. It all boils down to
control and power."

Dr. Kramer might have been discussing the case of
David Konkol, a senior at the College of St. Thomas in
St. Paul, Minnesota. In 1970 David was president of
the Resident Student Council, which had been critical of
the administration's decision on various campus issues.
In 1971 David wrote a letter reproaching the administration in which he said: "The administration at the
college is stagnated by bureaucratic pettiness, paternal-
ism and inefficiency." The Chicago *Daily News* quoted a
reply from the Dean of Students, William B. Malevich,
that stated: "Recently you wrote criticizing the college
administration's inability to make decisions. You are
wrong—the administration can make decisions. As proof
of this the administration has decided to cancel your
financial-aid for the coming year."

The loss of a $600 National Student Defense Loan, a
$700 grant from the college, and a $300 job in the college

library was the price David paid to learn that for some people education means conformity, servility, and silence.

The Roselle, New Jersey, Board of Education must view its learning facilities in much the same way as does the administration of St. Thomas' College. The New York *Post* reported in June 1972 that the board had voted to remove from the school library four books from a list recommended by the librarian and the administration. The books were: John Kenneth Galbraith's *The Affluent Society*, Robert Lekachman's *The Age of Keynes*, Leonard Beaton's *The Struggle for Peace*, and *Today's Ism's: Communism, Fascism, Socialism and Capitalism* by William Ebenstein. The board's president, John Everett, was quoted as saying, "I am a conservative and I will not apologize for being a book banner. . . . I will do anything I can to thwart permissive liberalism, and I'm quite proud of it. . . . I blue-penciled those books because I violently disagree with them, especially Galbraith and Keynes. . . . I deny their right to tell me that their theories are correct."

In addition to the *Post*'s coverage, articles about the board's censorship appeared in *The New York Times, Variety,* and *Newsletter on Intellectual Freedom,* among other publications. The case came to the attention of the Author's League of America. Mr. Mills Ten Eyck, Jr., executive secretary of the ALA, wrote to the board president, to the New Jersey Commissioner of Education, and to Governor William Cahill. The letter called the board's decision . . .

. . . an example of fear of the printed word, intolerance and a shocking disregard for the Constitutional
principles of free speech. It is incredible that adults
entrusted with the responsibility of administering a
public high school would engage in such an act of
book burning. . . .

What the Board and Mr. Everett obviously do not
understand is that the rights of free speech and press
were written into the Constitution to prevent ma-
jorities from restraining the distribution of books they
do not agree with—whether the majority be in Congress or a local school board.

Three weeks later the superintendent of schools in
Roselle, Robert F. X. Van Wagner, returned the banned
books to the reading list. He said he had read the four
books, found them unobjectionable, was putting in rush
orders for them. So the four books did return to the
Roselle High School library shelves, "balanced" by
volumes with a conservative point of view. No one who
appreciates the right to read could argue with Mr. Van
Wagner's decision. The students should have the opportunity to read books of all political persuasions. No
single group should be allowed to dictate what another
person may or may not read. But books are not the only
communications medium to be targets for vigilantes.

In February 1972 a Grosse Pointe, Michigan, movie
theater was showing *A Clockwork Orange,* an X-rated
film that presents the evils of violence. Only persons
eighteen years or older could see the film, so there was
no danger that immature minds would be poisoned by

the scenes of sex and violence. Yet the Grosse Pointe Motion Picture and Television Council decided it was their duty to close down the film. The organization's president was quoted in the Detroit *Free Press* as saying the film was brutal and sadistic. Then he added: "This is one of the best-produced and directed movies that I have ever seen. The acting and photography are superb. This is what makes it such a dangerous film."

The line of reasoning is difficult to follow. The movie's theme makes the point that violence threatens to destroy our civilization. If it is granted that the finished product is well-produced and directed, then that theme must have been developed successfully. Yet the Grosse Point Motion Picture and Television Council considered the film to be dangerous. Does that mean that the council is against any work of art that explores society's ills—that the council, in effect, is in favor of violence?

Obviously, this is not the council's feeling; the contradiction lies in its president's awkward attempt to justify the council's action. The council's goal is to decide what anyone over the age of eighteen should be allowed to see. Its members apparently believe they know better than anyone else in Grosse Point what is right and what is wrong. Their thinking is typical vigilantism. Possibly people in Grosse Pointe are willing to be ruled by vigilantes. There are other individuals, however, who consider themselves competent to make their own judgments.

One such strong-minded individual was the late H. L. Mencken, who commented at length on the foibles as well as on the magnificent potentialities of the United States. In 1971 Paul Shyre, a theatrical producer, director, and author, decided to adapt some of Mencken's writings into an evening of theater, much as Shyre had done earlier with Sean O'Casey's writings.

An appropriate theater for this play about Americana seemed to be Ford's Theatre in Washington, D.C., the scene of Abraham Lincoln's assassination by John Wilkes Booth. The theater had closed its doors not long after that tragic event. It had recently been reopened, however, as a restoration project of the National Park Service. The purpose behind the restoration was stated in the Ford's Theatre program for 1971–1972: "To impart to the visitor a feeling for the conditions that may have assailed the senses is to make history a personal experience and to humanize those who played the parts in days past."

An Unpleasant Evening with H. L. Mencken opened in the second week of March 1972, and the National Park Service labeled "objectionable" comments dealing with lynchings in the South and the quality of life in southern states. In short the organization wanted the script changed so there would be no reference to events that resembled those of Lincoln's day.

The March 18 Washington *Post* gave Paul Shyre's answer: "I'd close the show before I'd tamper with the script." Shyre said that there might be alterations in the show as it gets broken in, "but never under the pressure of censorship."

The National Park Service backed down when the incident received publicity, and Edwin Blacker, speaking for the organization, said the National Park Service was not censoring, but only suggesting. These suggestions were "not an order."

Thus a play that was about a man who loved America, and that was being performed in a theater where another patriot had been assassinated, was protected from pseudo-vigilantism by still a third strong-willed person and by national publicity in the news media.

Support in the fight against vigilantism can come from official government sources, too. Salt Lake City, Utah, prides itself on the city's cleanliness. The streets are spotless, and Salt Lake City would like the residents to be equally pure in their verbal usage, and so a city ordinance makes it unlawful to use "abusive, menacing, insulting, slanderous or profane language within the city limits of Salt Lake City." Mr. Robert Ray Davison was arrested during an altercation in a department store and charged under this ordinance. The city court promptly found him guilty.

Davison brought his case to the Utah District Court, and he won.

The government of Salt Lake City appealed to the Utah Supreme Court to overthrow the lower court's decision. It lost.

The Supreme Court ruled: "If the ordinance were held valid, one could be punished for swearing to himself if he should accidentally hit his thumb with a hammer."

But, unfortunately, there are pseudo-vigilante gangs who are not so easily defeated. These are the pressure groups, sometimes labeled "watchdog committees," that rise up when people feel that some official organization is not fulfilling its aim and therefore needs citizen surveillance. This brand of vigilantism appeals to malcontents as well as to people with real complaints who join because they want to feel they are finally doing something to protect themselves from a large, impersonal body. The weapon such groups most frequently employ is intimidation.

A suburban school district on the south shore of Long Island experienced this variety of pseudo-vigilantism. The district fits the qualifications for typical suburbia, as described in the earlier chapter on Suburban Vigilantism. Unexpected tax burdens had enraged many people so that they considered the school district an enemy. They formed a taxpayers' committee. The feeling of this taxpayer's watchdog group was that the high taxes must result from unnecessary expenditures or foolish purchases.

The first thing the group did was to organize guards who, at the close of school each day, could be found parked in their automobiles across from each of the district's schools. One longstanding rule that teachers employed by the district were expected to follow was that they should not leave the school building each day before 3:15 P.M. The ever-watchful parents association assiduously noted the name of any teacher who left the building before the scheduled time. Their purpose was to frighten any people they felt might be lax in their duties and who did not spend every salaried minute in the building. These angry residents would then descend upon the superintendent of schools, fact-laden clipboards clutched in their fists, and demand that the errant instructors be reprimanded and that disciplinary reports be put into their cumulative folders.

Children were used as spies in the classroom. Their parents ordered them to report any wasteful practices by teachers. Was every single page of every single workbook used before the books were discarded? Was construction paper or composition paper carelessly distributed? The resulting tension in certain of the district's classrooms seriously affected the learning situations.

The storm troopers for the watchdog committee would then bring their collected facts to the board of education member who had been elected on her promise to lower taxes. She turned this information into an exposé of wastefulness and used it as a weapon against the school budget suggested for the district.

The effect of this vigilante campaign was totally negative. School personnel from the superintendent to the custodian lived in daily fear of offending an Abigail-Williams-of-Salemlike child or some neurotic housewife. Teachers became angry. Though they spent all the required time in the buildings, many ceased to give that extra, unpaid effort that makes the big difference in a child's education. They did what they got paid to do, and that was all. The close relationship between many teachers and children weakened, and in some cases it died. Districtwide, the school budget was defeated that May.

Then more trouble came. The district was forced to operate under an austerity budget. Parents were dismayed to learn that there would be no school lunch program, no sports and no social activities, as these items were prohibited by the state from appearing in an austerity budget. Books and school materials would have to be purchased by each child. The extensive school bus schedule was cut back. Parents suddenly realized they would have to organize daily car pools to get their children to school.

When these facts had filtered through the community and been digested, another budget was called for. In piecemeal fashion, some of the cutbacks were installed separately. But even if the financial matters were slightly straightened out, the psychological effect on teachers and students would take years to heal. The pseudo-vigilantes may have won, but their children had lost.

Whenever any pseudo-vigilante group succeeds, there is always, somewhere, an equivalent loss. Though the battles are usually local and do not have the impact that Carry Nation's pseudo-vigilante battles had, the effects can be cumulative across the country. Each time a book is banned, each time a movie is closed down, each time some critic of society is silenced, another piece of freedom has been chipped away.

Afterword:
The Future of
Vigilantism

Few institutions seem to have as bright a future in America as vigilantism.

As we have seen throughout the book, underlying social tensions make themselves known in some form of violence. Repression only aggravates the tension, thus producing still more violence. Vigilantism rising to fight the violence is often met with counter vigilantism, which is equally destructive. If the problem could be visualized, it would look like a funnel-cloud, ever widening as it goes up and up.

There are no bumper sticker solutions to curb the tide of vigilantism. Individual and public awareness is the only really effective weapon that can be employed against it. Unfortunately, awareness is a slow, thoughtful process, usually the first victim in times of stress.

An awareness is needed first of all about the deceptive

forms that vigilantism may take. Consider the various types discussed in the last few chapters. Most of the vigilante groups were composed of people who sincerely believed that something was wrong. Many of their grievances were probably justified, but all the groups chose dangerous means to combat the problems. And the outcomes were rarely what had been hoped for or expected. The children of the suburban watchdog committee were deprived of the decent education they had been receiving. Heroin is still abundant on the C. W. Post campus. Rabbi Kahane claimed that the people who bombed Sol Hurok's office were insane; Kahane, however, must bear the moral responsibility for the deaths.

Vigilantes rarely suspect how far the results of their activities may extend. As Richard Maxwell Brown writes:

> The difficulty of frontier vigilantism is that it has no stopping place. Men accustomed to taking law into their hands continue to take law into their hands even after regular judicial processes are constituted. They continue to take the law into their hands right into these days. . . . They do not approve of a man or situation, and they cannot wait for the regular processes to assist their realizations. . . . So they burn down a ghetto, they loot and pillage, they bury three civil rights workers beneath a dam or they shoot a man in a caravan in Dallas or on a motel balcony in Memphis.
>
> —*Violence in America*

Another type of awareness is also needed today, and that is an understanding of a peculiar characteristic of the American people: an odd combination of apathy and militancy. Frequent accounts describe incidents where citizens witness terrible crimes and do nothing to help the victim. A mood of "not getting involved" seems to have settled over the country. On the other hand, a problem which touches an individual personally often produces feelings which demand that he make every effort, legal or not, to find a solution to it. We seem to have become interested only in what affects *us;* then we are likely to attack viciously.

The answer to apathy is not vigilantism but education. Every major problem in the country will eventually affect us all in some way. A means must be found to bring this message home to those citizens who today feel unconcerned.

Responsible citizens fear vigilante groups of all sorts because their increase reflects a loss of confidence in, and respect for, the country's legal institutions. Thinking people are agreed that a new respect is needed if we are to ward off social anarchy. Respect for *everyone,* from our next-door neighbor to the policeman on the beat to the President of the United States, must be regained.

There seems only one logical starting place—with the individual. The man who sat by his apartment window, listening to the screams of a woman being stabbed to death on the street below, must have felt pangs of conscience because he did nothing to help. The person who joins a vigilante band of any sort must in some quiet moment realize that his group is morally wrong in using fear and intimidation to bring about change. Even if the group's goal is a desirable one, there is always a better way, a legal way, to achieve it.

This self-awareness will have to extend to everyone. If the policeman on the block wants to be respected, then he, too, must develop self-respect. Those free meals or gifts of merchandise at Christmas are only a different form of bribery than his superiors may be receiving from leaders of organized crime.

Politicians should stop speaking and acting as if the loss of respect in them is solely the fault of their constituents. When even deputies of the President of the United States are accused of acting as political vigilantes because of illegal spying on the opposition, as they were in the Watergate Case, is it any wonder that the nation's faith in the honesty of its elected officials has diminished? The people's trust in government was not stolen but squandered away. Now, like a wasted fortune, it can only be restored by slowly building it up again penny by penny.

Without a return to self-respect, and respect for our institutions, vigilantism will no doubt flourish. The conditions of crime and fear are too prevalent and too many people are becoming increasingly frightened for excessive measures not to be attempted. If the trend continues, the ultimate form of vigilantism in America could conceivably come about—the election of a vigilante to run the country.

Mile-long phalanxes of citizens ready to support practically anybody who promises means to return safety to their homes are about to form. If no rational help comes soon, can irrational demagogic leadership be far behind?

—*The Village Voice*
October 12, 1972

Yet there are hopeful signs. A growing sense of the importance and worth of the individual as well as a greater awareness of social and political problems can be seen all about us. Hopefully, this new insight will lead people to more reasonable methods of dealing with these situations. The country will then be able to take better stock of its past mistakes and move forward to a more enlightened and equal system of justice, rather than backward to vigilantism.

Sources and
Suggested Reading

RESOURCES RELATED TO CHAPTERS

CHAPTER 1. THE THREAT OF COLONIAL LIVING

Andrews, Charles M. *The Colonial Period of American History*. New Haven: Yale University Press, 1934.

Brown, Richard Maxwell. *The South Carolina Regulators*. Cambridge: Harvard University Press, 1963.

Parrinder, Geoffrey. *Witchcraft*. Baltimore: Penguin Books, 1958.

CHAPTER 2. THE THREAT OF FRONTIER LIVING

Bancroft, Hubert H. *Popular Tribunals*. New York: McGraw-Hill, 1967.

Caughey, John W. *Their Majesties the Mob*. Chicago: University of Chicago Press, 1960.

Coke, Henry J. *A Ride Over the Rocky Mountains to Oregon and California*. London, 1852.

Dimsdale, Thomas J. *Vigilantes of Montana*. Norman: University of Oklahoma Press, 1953.

CHAPTER 3. THE FRUIT OF ECONOMIC CHANGE

Coblentz, Stanton A. *Villains and Vigilantes*. New York: Thomas Yoseloff, 1957.
Roske, Ralph J. *Everyman's Eden*. New York: Macmillan, 1968.
Selvin, David F. *The Other San Francisco*. New York: Seabury Press, 1969.
Stewart, George. *The Committee of Vigilance*. New York: Ballantine Books, 1971.

CHAPTER 4. THE THREAT OF SOCIAL CHANGE

Chalmers, David M. *Hooded Americanism*. Garden City: Doubleday, 1965.
Dixon, Thomas, Jr. *The Clansman*. New York: Grosset & Dunlap, 1905.
Gillette, Paul J., and Eugene Tillinger. *Inside the Ku Klux Klan*. New York: Pyramid, 1965.
Simcovitch, Max. "The Impact of Griffith's Birth of a Nation on the Modern Ku Klux Klan," *The Journal of Popular Film*, Winter 1972, pp. 45–54.

CHAPTER 5. THE THREAT OF CHANGING MORAL CLIMATE

Taylor, Robert Lewis. *Vessel of Wrath*. New York: New American Library, 1968.

CHAPTER 7. TODAY: RURAL VIGILANTES

Sprague, W. D. *Case Histories from the Communes*. New York: Lancer Books, 1972.

CHAPTER 8. TODAY: SUBURBAN VIGILANTES

"Statement of Findings of Fact and Determination and the Order" Pfaus *vs.* McDonough, Department of Law and Public Safety, State of New Jersey, August 16, 1968.

CHAPTER 9. TODAY: URBAN VIGILANTES

Black, Jonathan. "Block Power—The Jane Street Story," *The New York Times*, May 7, 1972.
"Constitution and By-Laws," New Jersey Civil Mobile Patrol, Inc., Essex County, New Jersey, March 22, 1965.

CHAPTER 10. TODAY: POLITICAL, RACIAL, AND RELIGIOUS VIGILANTES

"Bully Tactics." *Newsweek*, LXXVII (January 18, 1971), p. 34.
Cleaver, Eldridge. *Soul on Ice*. New York: McGraw-Hill, 1968.
Kahane, Meir. *Never Again*. New York: Pyramid, 1972.
Marine, Gene. *The Black Panthers*. New York: New American Library, 1969.
"New Tension Between Russia and U.S." *U.S. News & World Report*, LXX (January 25, 1971), pp. 20–21.
"Private Jewish War on Russia." *Time*, XCVII (January 25, 1971), p. 18.

CHAPTER 11. TODAY: PSEUDO-VIGILANTES

American Library Association. *Newsletter on Intellectual Freedom*, XX, No. 4 (July 1971) and No. 6 (November 1971).
Authors League of America, Inc. "The President's Report," August 24, 1972.

OTHER PERIODICAL RESOURCES

The following newspapers and publications were also extremely helpful in providing information for this book:

The Breeze (Philadelphia)
C. W. Post *Pioneer* (New York)
Los Angeles *Times*
New York *Post*
The New York Times
Newsday (New York)

Philadelphia *Bulletin*
Publishers' Weekly (New York City)
San Francisco *Chronicle*
San Francisco *Examiner*
Schenectady *Gazette* (New York)
Variety (New York City)
The Village Voice (New York City)

OTHER SOURCES

GENERAL READING

Brown, Richard Maxwell. *American Violence.* Englewood Cliffs, New Jersey: Prentice-Hall, 1970.

Demaris, Ovid. *America the Violent,* New York: Cowles Book Co., 1970.

Forman, James A. *Law and Disorder.* New York: Thomas Nelson, 1972.

Graham, Hugh Davis, and Ted Robert Gurr. *Violence in America.* New York: New American Library, 1969.

Packard, Vance. *A Nation of Strangers.* New York: David McKay, 1972.

FILM

Salem Witch Trials (27 min., b/w). Boston University Film Library (765 Commonwealth Avenue, Boston, Massachusetts 02215).

ORGANIZATIONS

American Library Association
50 East Huron Street
Chicago, Illinois 60611

(Issues the *Newsletter on Intellectual Freedom.*)

Library
National Council on Crime and Delinquency
NCCD Center
Paramus, New Jersey 07652

Index